LOBBYING ON A SHOESTRING

A Publication of
The Massachusetts Law Reform Institute

LOBBYING ON A SHOESTRING

Second Edition

JUDITH C. MEREDITH

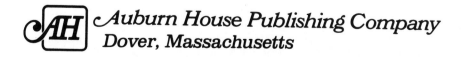

Auburn House Publishing Company
Dover, Massachusetts

Copyright © 1989 by Massachusetts Law Reform Institute.

Library of Congress Cataloging in Publication Data
Meredith, Judith C.
    Lobbying on a shoestring / Judith C. Meredith.—2nd ed.
      p.   cm.
    Includes index.
    ISBN 0-86569-190-8
    1. Lobbying—United States—States—Citizen participation—Handbooks, manuals, etc. 2. Lobbyists—United States—States—Handbooks, manuals, etc.   I. Title.
JK2498.M47   1989
328.73'078'0202—dc20   89-15028
                                              CIP

Printed in the United States of America

ACKNOWLEDGEMENTS

This book is an update and expansion of *Lobbying on a Shoestring* by Judith C. Meredith and Linda Myer, published by the Massachusetts Poverty Law Center in 1982. It grew out of a handbook written for participants in a legislative advocacy training conference in 1979 by Terrence McLarney, Rochelle Lefkowitz, Robert Schaffer, Kathleen O'Grady, Robert James, Arlene Sen, Mary Kay Leonard, Maureen Holland, and others.

For work on the current version, thanks go to my husband, Peter Rider, for his invaluable critique of the early drafts; to Hugh Munoz for the new charts and graphics; and to Allan Rodgers for his infinite faith in the project.

JUDITH C. MEREDITH

CONTENTS

CHAPTER 5

Floor Action

CHAPTER 8
Using the Media in a Legislative Campaign 135
by Linda Myer

LOBBYING ON A SHOESTRING

INTRODUCTION

Unlike the Ten Commandments, our laws were not carved in stone. While the Author of the Commandments apparently saw no need for future amendments, those who drafted the United States Constitution both provided a framework for national and state laws and created a way to change those laws and the Constitution itself. Although changes in the law must be approved by the appropriate legislative bodies, citizens can both instigate changes in the law and affect the outcome of the legislative process by exerting influence over their elected representatives—that is, by lobbying.

Lawmaking takes place on two levels. First, the United States Congress, which is made up of the Senate and the House of Representatives, has the power to write and amend the federal law. All 435 members of the House must stand for election every two years. A senator is elected for a six-year term; every two years a third of the 100 senators are up for election. Second, each state has its own constitution describing a legislative body similar to Congress. A state legislature has the power to write state law as long as it does not conflict with federal law. In Connecticut there is a General Assembly; in California, a State Legislature; in Massachusetts, The Great and General Court. In all 50 states the legislative body is composed of individuals who must stand for election or re-election every few years.

While each state's political structure may accommodate regional differences or geographical limitations, there is relative uniformity in legislative organization and procedures. In the end, each legislative body organizes itself into some sort of leadership structure, develops rules governing debate and voting procedures, and sets a meeting schedule. Eventually everybody meets in a large room where the members take turns proposing specific changes in the law, argue back and forth for a while, vote one way or another, and go on to the next proposal. At some point they decide they have finished and go home. It's all pretty simple when you get down to it.

1

Lobbying on a Shoestring was written to help individuals and organizations who want to change the law in their state. Neighborhood organizations, parent groups, citizen or consumer organizations, unions, professional associations, and advocacy groups regularly try to change the law. Some are trying to figure out how to go about this task.

How Lobbyists Are Born

The members of these lobby groups are usually ordinary citizens who have been directly affected—even hurt by—the application of an existing state law or by the absence of any law protecting them. By the time these folks decide that the only way to remedy their problem is to change the law, they are often angry, frustrated, and anxious: angry because they or someone they know has been harmed; frustrated because other attempts have failed to resolve the problem; and anxious because this business of "lobbying" is a new and unfamiliar game. Even the word "lobbying" conjures up an image of a slick, high-priced lawyer lobbyist whispering in the ear of a key politician to whom he has contributed thousands of dollars.

As a matter of fact, the author is a medium-priced professional lobbyist, representing human service professional and provider associations, parent and tenant organizations, and various advocacy groups, including legal services. I am not a lawyer, but I do my share of whispering with key legislators and regularly make modest contributions to their re-election campaigns.

Like many women in this business, I started as a volunteer. I belonged to an adoptive parent group. We had decided to "do something" about an existing law that forbid the adoption of children across religious lines. Through our parent support network we had learned that more than a thousand children, legally free for adoption, were "stuck" in foster care. While many of these kids were considered hard to place because they were older, handicapped, mixed-race, or part of a sibling group, the main stumbling block seemed to be the adoption agencies' unwillingness to place a child in a home where the religion was different from that of the birth mother. It was against the law, we were told.

Even though we did not believe that the religious background of the birth mother should have such a disproportionate weight in placement decisions, we tried for a time to assist in recruiting families with the correct religious credentials. It soon became painfully apparent that eager families with minority, mixed, or no religious background could never even be considered for the waiting children. If only the law could be changed!

Of course the law could be changed. I agreed to chair the legislative committee, and was lucky on three counts. I had a good state representative who helped draft the legislation and told me what to do and when. I had the membership list of my adoptive parent group and was able to build an enthusiastic network of folks who were were willing and able to talk to their own representatives. Finally, the organization raised money to pay for phone, postage, and child care so that some of us could spend some time at the State House.

It was frightening and frustrating moving around the State House with all those important and powerful looking people, but we kept bumping methodically from step to step. Eventually we won, and the sweetness of that victory is just as fresh today as it was in 1972. We had actually changed a bad law and enabled hundreds of children to be freed for adoption. We felt good. And powerful!

During that effort, we were given booklets and charts usually entitled, "How a Bill Becomes Law," describing the three-reading process in Massachusetts. But, I yearned to find the real book, one with the title, "How the State House Really Works." Such a publication would reveal the secrets I suspected were shared only by the legislators, lobbyists, and staff who seemed to be forever huddling and whispering to each other in the corridors. Years later, after participating in thousands of corridor conferences convened by boredom and dominated by idle gossip, a fellow lobbyist told me what he had said to a staff person as they watched me walk by during that first campaign.

"What do you hear?"

"Not much."

"Who's that woman over there with the kids? She's been around a lot lately."

"Something to do with kids stuck in foster care. She's got a bill in Ways and Means."

"Any chance?"

"I dunno, we got some letters. With pictures! This family in the district has a housefull. My guy's sold."

"Do you think I could get him if I sent in some pictures of cute bankers?"

"As long as they're not mug shots."

I stopped looking for the "How the State House Really Works" book when I finally figured out that there were no secrets. Only a long list of planning and organizing activities, all adding up to what is called a lobbying campaign.

Rules of the Game

There are two rules of lobbying which provide the foundation of the citizen-network model outlined in this book. The rules are little more than observations of human nature within the context of the political arena and all its peculiarities, but they have been proved over and over in hundreds of campaigns. They are: (1) Elected and appointed officials make different decisions when watched by the affected constituents; and (2) lobbying is simply getting the right information to the right people at the right time.

Rule 1. Elected and appointed decision makers make different decisions when watched by the affected constituents.

Imagine that you are a legislator about to vote on a bill which would force manufacturers to install very expensive filtering devices onto their waste water discharge pipes. Your district is downriver from a large mill and you have received many letters, phone calls, and petitions from the voters in your district urging you to vote for the filter bill and clean up the old swimming holes. You were all set to vote for the bill until you met with mill management and union representatives, who claim that the high cost of the filters would force the plant to close a division and lay off 200 workers from your district.

Now imagine that you are another legislator about to vote on the same bill. There is no such plant near your district fouling the local swimming holes. You don't hear anything from anybody in the district, but lobbyists from a state-wide industrial association stop by with a 20-page briefing paper describing how similar laws in other states have forced dozens of businesses to close and lost thousands of jobs.

You don't need a degree in political science to know that, in the first instance, the poor devil caught between affected constituents has a difficult decision to make. And it will be a very different decision than his colleague will make after he reads—or does not read—all that material from the association.

Rule 2. Lobbying is simply getting the right information to the right person at the right time.

Legislators have too much work to do. Really. In Massachusetts, for example, over 8,000 bills are filed every year and 15 to 20 new items appear on the calendar every formal session. It is virtually impossible for a legislator to do personally all the research necessary to cast a fully informed vote on 15 brand new bills every session. Legislators listen to trusted colleagues who have expertise, to committee research staff, to their own staffs, to lobbyists on both

Rule I: Elected and appointed decision makers make different decisions when watched by the affected constituents.

Rule II: Lobbying is simply getting the right information to the right person at the right time.

sides of the issue, and last—but definitely not least—to voters from their district. Voters from the district who are informed and organized enough to talk with their legislators before the vote have the most power and influence in the entire process.

Keys to a Winning Campaign

The key elements of a winning lobbying campaign are:

1. A committee authorized to plan the campaign, to assign and carry out specific tasks, to evaluate and readjust strategies and tactics along the way, and to organize and coordinate grass-roots membership activities in support of the campaign.
2. An official lobbyist (paid or volunteer) with good interpersonal skills who knows or can learn the procedural rules and who can spend the necessary time in the state house.
3. Enough money to pay for the expenses of organizing the network, including postage, printing, phone, and maybe even a salary for the lobbyist.

Success depends almost entirely on the campaign's ability to mobilize a network of individuals to lobby their own legislators with letters, phone calls, and meetings in the district. Legislators appreciate a good lobbying campaign that presents accurate, timely information, and they respond to a campaign that presents that information through real voters from the district. In fact, timely, informed constituent contact is so rare that five letters from constituents and another set of phone calls is considered enough "heat from the district" to keep most legislators on course.

Some Advice

Many parts of this book use the legislative process of Massachusetts to illustrate the general principles of building and executing an effective lobbying campaign and to provide anecdotal evidence of what should or should not happen when using any of the suggested lobbying tactics. "Boston Pols" have a long rowdy history going back to the American Revolution and the Boston Tea Party. They have been practicing politics by overthrowing each other ever since. They're so good at it that when they get bored they either run around the country calling themselves political consultants, or they rewrite their rules to make them a little harder for newcomers to understand. The procedures in the Massachusetts House and Senate are very likely to be more complicated than those in other states. Readers from more sensible states can take comfort in that.

Readers planning a lobbying campaign in Massachusetts or in any other state should not use this book as their sole authoritative source; rather they should go to their state house book store and get also an up-to-date rule book prepared for their state.

Keep in mind that all fifty states embrace the same checks and balances that are embodied in the United States Constitution. For instance, all states except Nebraska have bicameral (or two-branch) legislatures. Although the particular names, dates, places, and rules may differ from state to state, all the state legislatures (including Nebraska):

- are elected;
- are organized into hierarchical leadership schemes;
- are organized further into specialized-issue committees that hold some sort of hearing on bills;
- have at least one committee more powerful than all the others, with control over the appropriation process;
- have rules that govern the legislative agenda, the length of debate, and the postponement of debate;

A lobbyist is born.

- must either have gubernatorial approval to enact laws or must override the Governor's disapproval;
- have a clerk's or a counsel's office where petitions and bills are filed and where any question can be asked (though not always completely answered); and
- have one room somewhere where copies of bills and the day's agenda can be found.

Finally—have fun! The process and the players can be goofy, but most politicians are, by profession, charming and colorful. Resist taking them, or yourself, too seriously. And remember, significant changes in public policy have been made by individuals and small groups with determination, tenacity, and a sense of humor.

Chapter 1

LAYING THE GROUNDWORK
FOR A SUCCESSFUL CAMPAIGN

Asked whether he knew a path through the intimidating Alps, Hannibal is supposed to have said, "We will find a way or we will make one." That's how you should view the task of putting together all the elements of a successful lobbying campaign. But before you begin, you should decide whether your bill addresses a public or a nonpublic issue.

Public and Nonpublic Issues

Most of the bills considered in a legislative session address **nonpublic issues;** that is, the only people who care enough about these bills to work on them, to understand them, or even to read them are the special interests affected by them and their supporters in the legislature. Every year these bills advance the causes of everyone from public utilities trying to get rate hikes to animal lovers hoping to outlaw leghold traps.

Rarely are these bills debated in the legislature or covered in the press. They are decided by simple voice votes. Usually, most members have read only the bill's title as it appears on the calendar— unless, of course, someone has "lobbied" them in support of the bill. The bill may still pass on a voice vote without debate, but a team of legislators who understand the bill are ready to head off any attempts to kill it.

About 10 percent of the bills debated in state legislatures address **public issues,** or any issue controversial enough to be covered on a regular basis by the major media. Every reasonably informed citizen knows something about the current public issues and probably has a strong opinion about the proposed solutions. Abortion, capital punishment, gay rights, and property taxes all are examples of public issues. Hunting and fishing rights of Native Americans have been fiercely debated in the states of Washington and Maine. Industrial states such as New Jersey, New York, and Massachusetts struggle with toxic waste dumps and polluted beaches.

Sometimes a nonpublic issue turns into a public issue midway through the legislative process because the press starts covering it or because the legislative debate is extraordinarily dramatic, compelling, or timely. For example, Proposition 13 in California captured the attention of the nation as well as California voters in 1978, leading to an epidemic of property tax limitation campaigns in dozens of states. The annual dull debate on solid waste disposal livened up in New Jersey when bags of used hypodermic needles washed up on the Atlantic City boardwalk. Anti-nuclear activists in Massachusetts trying to mobilize public opposition to local nuclear power plants got a big boost in the wake of the Chernoble disaster.

Often, inexperienced lobbyists think the only way to pass a bill is to build it up in the press and turn it into a public issue. But this strategy has disadvantages. A public issue is no longer yours to control. The timetable gets speeded up, opponents crawl out of the woodwork, and new influential champions in the press and the legislature come forward with their own ideas for compromise and coalition. If you do wake up some morning to find your nice little manageable campaign on the front pages, take a deep breath, inventory your resources and your research, and get everybody ready for some fast action. It *could* happen to you!

For example, over a period of years, consumer advocates in Massachusetts lobbied vainly for auto insurance reform. While their arguments were strong, so were those from the insurance actuaries, the trial lawyers, and the auto body shops. It was all too confusing, conflicting, and complicated for ordinary mortals to understand—until they got their new insurance bills. An enraged public brought the nonpublic debate on auto insurance reform to a fast conclusion with a short, pointed message to the legislature: "Do something. Now!"

Fortunately, the consumer organizations had the technical research all done and the networks in place. Skilled with the media and respected in the Legislature, they moved quickly to establish themselves as spokespersons for consumers and offered specific legislative solutions. When the consumer organizations mobilized their networks, they galvanized public opinion as well. They

Try not to arouse unnecessary opposition.

achieved in a few months what they had been working toward for five years—real auto insurance reform.

Once you know whether your issue is a public or nonpublic one, you can plan your campaign. For nonpublic issues you will try to work quietly with individual legislators and not draw a lot of attention from potential opposition or the press. When lobbying a public issue you must learn how to deal with new opposition as well as new supporters (who can be very trying), all under the brutal scrutiny of the press. The main difference between the two campaigns is in the use of the press. (See Chapter 8.)

Advance Planning of the Campaign

For both kinds of issue, advance planning is the key to success. It's important to have a rough plan of the entire campaign at the beginning, rather than biting off chunks as they come up. Once the legislative session begins, events roll quickly. If you wait until the day before the committee hearing to plan a hearing strategy, you will lose your opportunity to call up all the witnesses you need. Successful lobbying campaigns include the same sort of tasks that should be done in advance, and responsibility for each of those tasks should be assigned to a specific person or committee.

The Lobbying Campaign Committee

The campaign committee is responsible for developing a plan for who does what and when. Information must be gathered, lists made, experts consulted, and workplans developed, modified, and modified again. The best time to organize such a committee is several months before the legislative session begins, but ad hoc committees have self-organized in the middle of a crisis and done very well.

Instant credibility is granted when the committee names itself and prints up stationery. "The Coalition to Liberalize Adoption" letterhead illustrated on page 21 was produced on a home computer and reproduced on a borrowed office copying machine.

Unincorporated informal coalitions of volunteer citizen lobbyists don't have to register as lobbyists in most states, even if they spend a modest amount of their members' money producing printed lobbying materials. However, many states have established spending ceilings for such unregistered citizen lobbyists, and every state has some law requiring paid lobbyists and their employers to register and file reports. Check it out with your secretary of state.

The Base

The base is an organized or organizable group of persons who care enough about the issue to talk to their own elected representatives about it. These are the **affected constituents** referred to in Rule 1. Legislators do make different decisions when watched by the affected constituency.

It is almost impossible for a legislator to say no to a request by a delegation of affected constituents from his or her own district—especially if the constituents are registered voters. By organizing the base you can establish a presence at the state house that can turn the legislator's reluctance to say no into a positive commitment to support your bill. Ways to create that presence and its subsequent pressure are discussed in more detail throughout this book. Briefly, they include:

- organizing letter writing campaigns to all legislators from their constituents;
- arranging meetings with legislators and constituents;
- presenting good testimony at the committee hearing;
- developing and using a "phone tree" (a list of people who will call others, who will call others) to remind legislators of their commitments the day before the vote;
- having observers in the gallery to watch the vote; and
- writing thank you notes after the vote.

Training the members of your base to do these tasks effectively is key to developing an enthusiastic and powerful legislative network. (See the training activities section later on in this chapter.)

The Lobbyist

There are two kinds of lobbyists in the state legislature: volunteers and professionals. Don't assume that professional lobbyists are always more successful than volunteers. Volunteers are often more convincing—especially if they are tenacious, persevering, and cheerful—and their issue is compelling.

The lobbyist's job is to put Rule 2 (getting the right information to the right person at the right time) into action. The lobbyist must coordinate the flow of information between the legislative sponsors of the bills, the members of the grassroots base, the legislative leadership, and any possible opponents. This is not technically difficult—just tedious.

There are two major pitfalls the lobbyist must avoid: losing the confidence of the base and losing the confidence of the legislators.

It is the base's solid support of the campaign plan that creates the lobbyist's "clout" with legislators in the first place. Smart lobbyists spend half of their time building the base and fine-tuning the legislative network, making it a little bigger and stronger every day.

Constant careful briefings on unfolding developments will necessitate regular late-night conference calls for committee members and the lobbyist. Training sessions, regular updates, and legislative alerts through mailings or telephone trees will keep the network up to date. Information builds the network and builds the trust that will be needed when the inevitable happens—compromise. Laying out all the possible options along the way will avoid the typical fatal mistake of novice lobbyists: agreeing to compromise before adequate consultation with the decision-making committee.

Earning and keeping the confidence of legislators is simpler. All they want is somebody to tell them what a bill does, how much it costs, how many people in the district care about it, and who's against it and why. In 40 seconds. On one page. Over and over. Before they agree to support the bill. Before they testify at the hearing. Before they write a letter to Ways and Means. Before the floor debate. Before the vote. *Patience is a virtue.*

The Lawyer, the Expert

Persons who love the law or good sausage should not watch either one being made. (Bismark)

Both a legal advisor and a recognized expert in the subject area addressed by your bill are important members of your team. They can help you draft the bill, provide technical briefings to legislators and staff, present credible testimony at committee hearings, and advise you on the meanings and effects of amendments proposed later on in the process. Sometimes you can find within your own or allied organization an expert who will help you free of charge.

After drafting the bill, the expert and the lawyer can help find the answers to two questions: How much will this bill cost? Why is this proposed solution better than any others? The answers will be incorporated into fact sheets, press releases, and training materials.

Highly trained experts such as scientists and lawyers accustomed to logical and rational problem solving often have a difficult time working in lobbying campaigns. Look for persons with patience, humility, and a sense of the absurd.

The Money

Here is a way to put together a "shoestring" budget for a lobbying campaign. Try to estimate an expense for every activity described, basing it on the number of people on your mailing list and the real need for expenses for your lobbyist and committee members.

Network Training Activities. Suggestions for training agendas and materials are outlined later in this chapter. Plan for a single state-wide meeting or several regional meetings. You will need a training package for everyone. Figure out what space, refreshments, and printing you can get for free and budget the rest. If you decide to build morale and create visibility, buttons are fun but homemade paper badges attached with common pins are cheaper.

Network Updating. Plan at least eight mailings to the entire membership list. Having a volunteer with a home computer ready to produce labels and maintain lists is wonderful, but file cards work just as well. You can skip the envelopes by designing a folded and stapled newsletter and save money by mailing most of the newsletters 2nd class. Do plan for at least two first-class emergency alerts.

Legislative Lobbying Materials. You should make enough copies of the original bill and the accompanying fact sheet to pass out to every member of the legislature, plus another 25 percent to be safe. As your bill proceeds through the process, update only the fact sheet to reflect any changes made. Amendments made in committee will be printed up as committee reports; amendments made in floor debate will be printed in the daily journals. Copy these amendments and attach them to your updated fact sheets.

This budget item is an incentive for short bills and single-page fact sheets, because printing can be very expensive. However, most state capitols have at least one cheap copying center close by, and your legislative sponsors can usually get a limited amount of emergency copying done free.

Extraordinary Expenses for the Committee and the Volunteer Lobbyist. These include child care, travel, and parking expenses related to training, and state house activities. Budget the lobbyist for one day a week during the session, plus another 20 days for crisis management. Committee members should be on standby for the 20 days as well. Long-distance phone bills will definitely increase for the lobbyist and the committee, and that budget will depend on your local rate structure. If you get lucky and find good enthusiastic volunteers who do not require reimbursement, you may count those blessings into your budget only if you choose them because they are good and enthusiastic and not because they are independently wealthy.

Paid Lobbyist. Hiring an experienced lobbyist to give your bill the "full treatment"—that is, to design the campaign, prepare the training and lobbying materials, set up the constituent meetings with legislators, coordinate the network activities, personally lobby key legislators, and so forth—can be expensive. Businesses often pay hundreds of thousands of dollars a year to lobbyists who combine earned knowledge and personal credibility with a support staff that does material production and distribution.

Those lobbyists who work with nonprofit, low-budget, volunteer membership groups prepare a plan that relies heavily on the resources of the group itself for material production and distribution and most of the legislative contact to achieve a more affordable price. For around $10,000 you could get a membership training package, regular consultation and advice for your volunteer lobbyist, and a dependable source for the informal but vital "state house gossip." The real benefit is accessibility to key legislators and staff who simply pay more attention to a new citizen campaign coming in under the wing of a respected and trusted professional. Fees will increase with the estimates of time spent designing the campaign or direct lobbying.

Ask legislators and staff people knowledgeable about your issue which lobbyists they would recommend to handle your bill. Call them up and negotiate in a straightforward way. Many lobbyists make their money on a number of high-priced lobbying accounts and are willing to do a few campaigns that interest them relatively cheaply.

Mobilizing Your Base

The lobbyist must begin a filing system that will gradually develop into two very important lists: (1) all the legislators and key staff, and (2) your legislative network members.

Legislators and Key Staff

This list will track each legislator's current position on your bill and identify his or her staff member who is doing the work. (After a few months of lobbying, you will appreciate the humor in the preceding sentence.) In the state capitol you will find the official list of all the legislators, with their phone and room numbers, their home address, and their district by city, town, ward, and precinct. Put that list on file cards or on a list you can carry around, and start keeping notes. Keep this confidential within the small campaign-organizing committee and your legislative sponsors. You shouldn't give potential opponents any information about your weak spots.

The Legislative Network

For a group lobbying on a shoestring, building this list is the most important job, and it's worth spending a lot of your resources to do

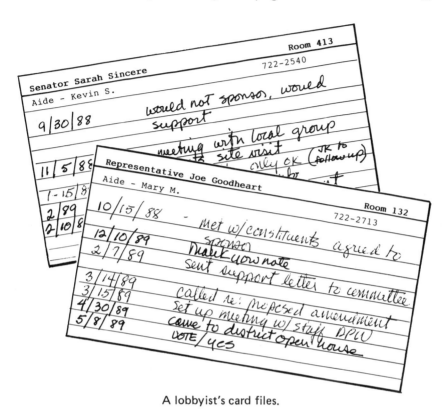

A lobbyist's card files.

it well. You are filing this legislation because there is a group of people who will benefit directly from the proposed change in the law. They are the affected constituency. Start there. *Every one of those people—and their friends and relatives—has a state representative and a state senator.* The goal is to find one voter in every representative's and senator's district who will organize phone calls and letters to his/her legislator on 24-hour's notice. There is no shortcut to this task. Start with the group members, their relatives and friends. Add allies as you find them. Keep building these names into telephone trees and mailing lists throughout the legislative campaign.

All network members should be asked to write or visit their legislators to tell them about their own interest in the bill and to ask for a commitment of the legislator's support. A report on this meeting and copies of letters exchanged should be forwarded to the lobbyist. New network people should know they will be taught how and when to communicate further with their legislators. Regular updates will keep them abreast of the campaign, and periodic legislative "alerts" through the mail or a phone tree will beg them to write or call one more time.

Organizing a Lobby Day

Many groups start their lists by organizing a "lobby day" at the State House. A lobby day is simply an organized method of getting a group of local network members into the state legislature on the same day to meet with each other and with their own representatives and senators. There are a number of worthwhile goals that can be accomplished simultaneously in a lobby day:

1. Network members can be organized according to their legislative districts, with a discreet series of tasks that introduce them to their roles as citizen lobbyists and to their own state representative and senator.
2. The organization can establish an identity at the legislature with the legislators and the media. Just thirty people with badges identifying them with a cause (such as "Save the Whales") will be noticed and talked about by reporters and members. And even if no reporter runs a story about you on the first occasion, the information will register in their memories; they'll remember you the next time you come around.
3. By meeting with people from around the state who share the same problem or cause, network members will get a sense of comfort, confidence, and power.
4. Network members will learn about the legislative process and will get to know and trust the legislative coordinator who will later send them legislative alerts with instructions to do something (writing or phoning, perhaps) *immediately.* This personal contact with the lobbyist makes it more likely that you will be able to elicit cooperation from network members throughout the campaign.

At least some representatives and senators will indicate where they stand on the issue, enabling the coordinator to begin the list of legislative supporters. Here are nine basic steps for organizing a lobby day:

1. Five weeks in advance, choose a day when the legislature will be in session.
2. Find a meeting room near the state capitol building or ask a legislator to reserve a room inside for briefing your own members. (A legislative sponsor will usually do this for you; see Chapter 2 on finding sponsors.)

On the way to a lobby day.

3. Notify your members of the planned lobby day and tell them to call their own representatives, senators, or staff aides to ask for a 10-minute meeting following the briefing session.
4. Prepare copies of fact sheets for all the network people who will be there and enough copies of the bill for all the legislators.
5. Prepare a press release announcing the lobby day to distribute to the state house press.
6. Make or buy identifying buttons or badges for all your network people. Just a three-inch homemade sign (fastened with a pin) stating your slogan ("Save Community Action" or "Support our Schools") gives you immediate visibility and camaraderie.
7. On lobby day hand out the buttons and fact sheets at the

preparatory briefing. Then the group leaders or the legislative sponsor should give the network people a strong pep talk. Remind them to report back to the briefing room after their meetings with legislators and make sure that they do it.

8. Have the network members visit their own representatives and senators, tell them their feelings about the bill, and leave their names and addresses, asking the legislators to drop them a note when they've made up their minds on the bill. Meanwhile, they should guess the legislator's probable position and report it back to the lobbyist in the briefing room.

9. Later the network members should write notes to their own reps and senators to thank them for their time and remind them of the urgency of the bill.

Network Training

A typical agenda for a training session is illustrated on page 21. Materials should include a copy of the bill; a fact sheet; a list of legislators with address and phone number; tips on writing letters, making phone calls, and setting up a meeting; and charts of the legislative process. (You are hereby given permission to copy these items from this book.)

Many people are intimidated by the idea of calling or writing their legislator. Reassure your legislative network members by teaching them how to do it right, by promising to keep them informed, and finally by revealing that they will have to carry out some sort of lobbying activity only about six times during the legislative session. Your goal for the training is to help the network members understand the power they are creating with their phone calls, letters, and lobby days. Construct your training around the two rules of lobbying and you will demystify the process and empower your network.

You may want to consider inviting your legislative sponsors to your training session. Enlightened legislators can help advance your goal of dymystifying the process by candidly sharing some of their past victories and misfortunes along the "How a Bill Becomes Law" chart. They can also help empower your network by endorsing the two rules of lobbying with some anecdotal evidence.

Assessing Your Opposition

There are two reasons for assessing the potential opposition to your bill: (1) you must judge whether your network and resources will be

```
========================================
        Coalition to Liberalize Adoption
             444 Massachusetts Street
                Boston, MA 02215
                 (617) 555-3285
_____

        ======================================
                        AGENDA
        ======================================


    1. Welcome and Introduction

            Christine Cox - President, Coalition to
            Liberalize Adoption


    2. How a Bill Becomes Law

            Jeff Beckett - Chair, Legislative Committee


    3. How to Talk With Your Legislator

            Hon. Joseph Goodheart - Member, House of
            Representatives


    4. Small Group - Role Playing

            Leaders:

            M. William Mays (Western District)

            Joyce Farley (Greater Boston District)

            Jack Cowell (Central District)

            Maria Aquiar (Northeast District)

            Katy Gene Munoz (Southeast District)


    5. Feedback and Network Assignments

            Jeff Beckett
```

A network training agenda.

adequate to defend your bill against the forces of your opponents; and (2) you must know your opponents' arguments so that you can present facts and figures to legislators that will blow these arguments out of the water. An ability to accurately present your opponents' views and your own counterarguments will help you dispute and defuse the opposition at committee hearings and floor debate.

There's an old lawyer's maxim: "Argue the law, but if the law is against you, argue the facts. If the facts are against you, attack your opponent." Follow only the first part of this maxim. The law (or lack of it) is against you; that's why you're trying to change it. But stick to arguing the facts. Don't attack your opponents with slander. It will only force them to take your campaign personally, and they'll fight you even harder.

Opposition comes from two places: outside the legislature and within it. The amount and force of the opposition depends on how controversial the bill is. Public issues usually generate more numerous and more forceful opponents than nonpublic issues do. Remember to list all the likely opposition, not just the most likely. Even if your list is long, don't be discouraged. Better to be prepared than be surprised.

Outside Opposition

To figure out who is likely to oppose your bill, look hard at what the bill does and whose interests it would limit. Don't quibble about whether their objections are reasonable or minor. Few things in life are certain, but you can bet that if your bill takes away existing privileges or sets limits where there were none before, someone is going to squawk.

For example, a bill requiring judges to make certain findings is bound to be opposed by some of those judges. In theory, most people agree that judges *should* be willing to do such things as part of their jobs. But many judges will oppose any change that makes more work for them or limits their discretion.

Even opposition that seems irrational to you can be serious. Judges, landlords, utility companies, merchants, and many other "establishment" individuals and groups have close personal friends in the legislature. Often, just a call or visit to their legislator friend will slow down or even kill your bill.

When you examine "the opposition" closely, you discover that they are a loose collection of groups and individuals with conflicting interests and ideas. Now ask yourself some questions about each element in this collection.

How Powerful Are They? Some groups are harder to oppose than others. For instance, the banking interests are probably the most powerful lobby in most states; the real estate and landlord interests, merchants, and judges are moderately powerful and effective at lobbying; and "fringe groups," such as the advocates of abolishing public financing of schools, may have only a narrow sphere of influence, and their effectiveness at lobbying varies widely from group to group.

Which Legislators Does Each Opponent Influence? Even a group that's relatively weak can thwart your bill if they have the ear of the right legislator—for example, the chair of the committee which will consider the bill. But usually influence over only one legislator, unless he or she holds a key position, has little effect on a bill.

How Hard Will They Fight on Your Issue? Even if a group has a lot of power over particular legislators, they may not fight hard against your bill. They may have other, more important, issues before the legislature at the same time. How can you find this out? Read their newsletters to discover their legislative agendas, and talk with friendly lobbyists, legislators, and reporters.

Is There Any Way to Cool Out the Opposition? Sometimes you can head off your opponents with an early compromise or agreement. Here, timing will be the key. Don't trade away components of your bill until you must. Prepare fallback positions ahead of time—but do not reveal or offer them until you see your bill's death looming large before your eyes. The best tactic is to listen to the opposition as closely as possible, but don't tell them anything at all. Keep your own counsel and don't draw any conclusions from what you see or hear.

If you must compromise, be sure to get a public commitment from your opponents to support and work for the deal *before shaking hands with them and walking away.* Or at least get them to promise that they won't oppose it. Often people make early compromises only to find their opponents working to dilute the bill later.

Opposition within the Legislature

Sometimes bills with little outside opposition have powerful opponents inside the legislature. Some legislators may consider your proposal simply a bad way of doing things. This attitude is typical of bills dealing with the reform of state government or (heaven forbid) of the legislature itself.

Most often, one or two powerful legislators may think that your bill sets a bad precedent or erodes a favorite public policy. This frequently happens on money issues. For example, every state capital has its own pack of "fiscal watch-dogs" who routinely oppose bills or budget amendments that purport to be "pilot programs," knowing full well that "pilot programs" have a way of ballooning into full-fledged bureaucracies. They see themselves as preventing abuses in state spending.

Inside opposition can sometimes be silenced or even turned around with a good campaign from affected constituents in the district. Pressure from legislator colleagues can be very persuasive as well.

Opposition from the Administration

If you resorted to filing a bill only after your organization tried and failed to convince state officials to change a policy or program, identifying your opposition within the administration is easy. You already know who they are and precisely why they will not or cannot solve your problem administratively. Newcomers should figure out which agencies their bill would affect and approach the agency through the official legislative liaison.

If the administration decides to publicly oppose your bill, their opposition will take the form of official testimony at the appropriate hearings and the circulation of materials documenting their position. They may even order their staff legislative liaison to lobby individual legislators and committee staff. The effectiveness of administration opposition depends on their credibility with the legislature and your ability to rebut their arguments. You can determine the administration's credibility by asking key committee staff and your legislative supporters. Sometimes administrative opposition can be helpful in winning the support of a committee chair engaged in a running feud with a commissioner; sometimes they're as thick as thieves.

If the administration has better things to do than launch a public campaign against your bill, you would be wise to try and document any opposition and prepare your rebuttal anyway. Many committees solicit written comments on pending legislation from the affected agency, and potential supporters will frequently ask, "What does the administration think of your bill?" Have your answers ready. As your bill gets close to the Governor's desk, you can be sure any administrative opposition will begin to move to stop or amend it. If you have already countered their arguments inside the legislature, you will be able to negotiate from strength to secure the Governor's approval.

Deal with administrative opposition in a straightforward and professional manner. When your bill becomes law, chances are you'll be working with the very same people during the implementation phase. (See Chapter 9, "Implementation Blues.")

Developing Allies

Allies, like opponents, are found both inside and outside the legislature. But there are different reasons for cultivating the two kinds of allies. Developing outside allies is part of the process of building a legislative network; developing inside allies is a way of searching for legislative sponsors.

Outside Allies—Building a Legislative Network

Building a legislative network for your campaign is much different from building a coalition. In a coalition, groups and individuals share a common view on a range of related problems and frequently share decision making as well. You are building a legislative network for a campaign. You make the decisions, and you must be free to build alliances with groups and individuals with whom you share nothing except a direct interest in getting your bill passed.

For example, utility companies may oppose bills preventing gas and electric shutoffs, but will support fuel assistance programs to pay gas and electric bills. The hospital association may oppose bills requiring hospitals to inform patients of rights or prohibiting certain collection practices, but may support a bill funding medical assistance programs for general relief recipients. Right-to-life groups in Massachusetts have worked hard to support adequate benefit levels for unmarried pregnant women.

Stretch your imagination. Keep asking yourself and others, "Who else should care?" Does your bill create jobs? If so, call the Chamber of Commerce and the labor organizations. Will your bill clean up the environment? Call the Audubon Society and the Sierra Club.

Invite allies to become part of your legislative network at the beginning of the campaign. Early endorsements of your bill from other well-known organizations will bring you borrowed credibility from those groups. Sometimes this will quickly win over uninformed or reluctant legislators.

Don't expect allies to use up much of their own power on your bill; they have their own legislative priorities. Their endorsement letter, testimony at the committee hearing, and general availability for last-minute lobbying are, however, tremendously useful. Also, full-time lobbyists working for your allied organizations are great sources of up-to-the-minute gossip, helpful hints, and advice on tactics.

Allies Inside the Legislature

Dying and going to heaven in politics means getting a good civil service appointment with no heavy lifting, except for the paycheck and the pension.

Dying and going to Heaven for a lobbyist is discovering that your little nonpublic bill is the exact solution to a problem that the chairman of the House Ways and Means committee has been trying to solve for years. It goes on his "must list." Anybody else who wants something out of his committee had better not oppose your bill; this includes even the Senate President, the Speaker of the House, and the Governor. Quickly and quietly your bill passes, either as a separate piece of legislation or as an addition to another bill. But one way or another, your nonpublic bill becomes law.

As we said, this is the lobbyist's version of Heaven. Until you get there, concentrate on finding other legislators and staff who have expertise or personal interest in the issue addressed by your bill and who believe it is good public policy.

Start with the joint committee that will first consider your bill. (See Chapter 2, Overview; and Chapter 4, Committees). Will the chairs of these committees support or sponsor it? Will any other influential committee members or staff support it? Then survey the membership to see who else might have a connection—personal, geographical, or professional—to the bill. Advocates for the disabled identify legislators who are disabled or who have a disabled family member. Proponents of day care concentrate on the young married legislators with children. Routinely ask your network members if they know anybody in the legislature. You, too, may find yourself speechless when a sweet elderly Sister of St. Joseph wonders if the Chairman of Ways and Means would remember his fourth-grade teacher who tutored him in arithmetic.

Mining for internal allies is a good way to recruit sponsors and to cultivate committee staff. Staff people usually have stored away great stockpiles of technical and political information. Usually they're happy to share what they know.

Avoid the "crazies." Every legislature has one or two members who are admittedly experts on an issue and may share your political views but are personally obnoxious, difficult to deal with, unpopular among the membership, and anathema to leadership. If you enlist them as sponsors (as they will undoubtedly press you to do), they will insist on leading debates and being your sole spokesperson with the press and with the legislative leadership. They ride like Don Quixote from fight to fight, always losing. It's difficult to avoid these people. But do so. Say "No." Say "Thank you," but say "*No.*" You must run your own campaign. You are looking for sponsors who:

- are respected for their political expertise and are well-liked by their peers;
- are in minor leadership slots or destined for them soon; and
- are willing to read your fact sheets and answer your questions.

It isn't necessary to get people who already know a lot about your bill and the problem it addresses. If these people exist, terrific,

It is permitted, in time of great trouble, to walk with the devil until you cross the next bridge.

that's like getting an unexpected scoop of ice cream on top of your slice of apple pie—delightful, but not essential. It's your job to educate your potential allies about the bill so that they can sell it to the rest of the membership. For this, they don't need much expertise on the issue. Their persuasion tactics with other legislators will probably go something like this:

> "Hey, Jack. I'd like your vote on this one. Stops whale hunting."
> "Whale hunting! Since when do you care about whales? You're from the Berkshires, for cripe's sake."
> "Hey, Jack—it's my bill. I got all these nuts and berries people in my district. They care—I care."
> "All right, all right. You got my vote. Think I got a couple of letters on that myself."

In your search you may find some powerful legislators who are enthusiastic about supporting your bill, but their legislative record and reputation on other issues are offensive to your organization's views. Frankly, identification with your citizen campaign is just what these legislators need to "lighten up" their public image, so they are willing and able to guarantee quick action in certain key committees. You also begin to hear from some nervous mainstream legislators: "Good grief, if those hardbars are supporting it, maybe you guys aren't just a bunch of goo-goos after all!"

When mining for allies, remember this old Bulgarian proverb: "It is permitted, in time of great trouble, to walk with the devil until you cross the next bridge."

Allies in the Administration

Allies inside the administration can establish credibility for a new lobbying campaign by developing and sharing data that confirm the unmet needs and by preparing a realistic cost analysis. If your inside allies lack credibility with key legislators, they can still turn the data over to you for inclusion in your back-up materials.

Sometimes administrative allies are so thrilled at having an outside constituent group working to get them more bureaucratic turf that they overpower the campaign with their expertise and resources. Well-meaning offers of free conference space or access to copying machines don't have to be refused, but you should resist depending on administration attorneys or other technical experts. It is particulary important to protect your campaign's identity during final negotiations with the legislature. Be prepared to gently remind administrative allies whose bill it is, anyway.

Chapter 2

LIFE IN THE LEGISLATIVE ARENA

You and your group have decided to embark on a legislative campaign. Your issue is compelling, your list of supporters is long, your research has uncovered only mild opposition, and you have decided that you have enough resources to fund and staff a respectable effort. Now it's time to take a closer look at the arena where this campaign will be fought. The next few chapters describe the formal structure and processes in one legislature and suggest specific strategies and tactics that can be used to affect the outcome of the decision-making process in any legislature.

Your first assignment is to collect all the official publications describing the leadership structure and the process and the attendant deadlines for filing and reporting of legislation. Read it all, and find two or three good people who work at the state house (legislators, lobbyists, or staff) willing to talk it all through with you. It is critical that you understand the formal structure and processes: Success depends on your ability to keep moving your campaign forward in a straightforward way.

Soon enough you will begin to pick up bits of information that suggest the existence of a back door to the formal process—that is, another informal leadership based on interpersonal friendships and organizational loyalties and traditions. The press and new insider friends you will meet in the state house will make much of these informal power networks. The most ordinary and predictable events will be explained away by ancient feuds, complicated conspiracies, or secret alliances. While these stories are always fascinating, they intimidate and distract newcomers who should be concen-

Novice lobbyists taking a closer look.

trating on building their support inside and outside the legislature rather than relying on shortcuts based on the latest conspiracy theory which, in turn, was based on yesterday's gossip.

Rookie lobbyists can't afford to get fancy. While there are a thousand ways to delay or amend a bill, there is only one way to get one passed—through the formal public process. Leave no stone unturned in your campaign and you will find yourself engaged in enough unexpected alliances and calculated conspiracies to write your own book.

Overview of a Legislature and How to Affect It

Profile of a Legislature

The Massachusetts legislature, like those in forty-eight other states, has two branches: the House and the Senate. Nebraska has a unicameral legislature, that is, a single legislative body.

The Massachusetts House is composed of 160 elected representatives, and the Senate has 40 elected senators. Both representatives and senators are elected every two years, in the even-numbered years.

Both branches meet at the State House in Boston. The annual session begins on the first Wednesday in January every year. It ends when both branches vote to go home for the year, and the Governor agrees. This is known as **prorogation.** (See Chapter 5 for more on prorogation.) Although there is no fixed date for prorogation, usually it occurs no earlier than mid-July because it takes that long to pass the state budget. The budget must be completed before the new fiscal year begins on July 1st, but in recent years the Governor has received it several days late.

Once the budget is passed, the legislature can prorogue. In election (even-numbered) years, legislators are preoccupied with their re-election campaigns, so the push for prorogation begins right after the Governor signs the budget.

If the legislature fails to prorogue by the day before the next annual session is slated to begin (first Wednesday in January), the old session dissolves automatically to make way for a new session. Whenever the legislature dissolves, most bills still before it die. Only bills refiled by the first Wednesday of the preceding December are dealt with in the new session. Many lobbyists still working to pass a bill in late November will file that bill again (called a **refile**) just in case it fails in the current session.

Members

Both senators and representatives are called legislators. Candidates for state representative must be at least eighteen years old and must reside in the district they seek to represent for one year prior to the election. Senators must also be at least eighteen, must reside in the Commonwealth for five years before election, and must reside in their district when elected.

Supreme Court rulings require the districts to be nearly equal in population. Each representative represents approximately 36,000 people, and each senator approximately 145,000 people. The legislature resets district boundaries when the federal census is taken.

Legislators receive a salary of $30,000 a year (in 1989), plus travel allowance. Leadership positions pay more. Many rank and file legislators, particularly those with families, have part-time jobs. Every rank-and file legislator has one personal aide and a part time secretary. Committee chairpersons have additional staff to do research and analysis, as do most members of the leadership team.

Much of the daily work of legislators involves fulfilling the immediate needs of their constituents. Most personal staff aides spend all their time responding to constituents' questions, requests, and complaints.

Democrats have dominated both branches of the Massachusetts legislature since Tip O'Neill became the first Democratic Speaker of the Massachusetts House in 1949. By 1989 the Republican party ranks were reduced to 7 members out of 40 in the Senate, and 31 out of 160 in the House.

Leadership

The Omnipotent Speaker of the House and Senate President. The House Speaker and Senate President are extremely powerful. *Unlike the U.S. Congress and some other state legislatures, there are no members of the Massachusetts legislature who hold positions of authority independent of the direct or indirect control of the House Speaker or the Senate President.* The Speaker and President can appoint and remove *all other members* from desirable positions at will—floor leaders, committee chairs, and committee members. So these two leaders have tremendous power over members who hold, or hope to hold, these positions.

Rules reforms enacted by both branches in the mid-1980s mandated that the President and the Speaker must bring their nominees for leadership posts and committee chairs before an open caucus of the Democratic members. It was hoped that this reform would help the President and the Speaker refrain from blatant cronyism and nominate persons who would have to be more responsive to the rank and file. In fact, caucus ratifications are routine in both branches, and there have been no attempts by any dissenting members to challange any nomination.

The Speaker and the President are both formally elected by a majority of their respective memberships. In practice each branch convenes party caucuses where the Democrats elect their nominee and the Republicans elect their nominee. Later, in formal House and Senate sessions, the Democratic nominees win because they have the votes. The losing nominees become the official Minority Leaders. Because Speakers and Presidents as well as Minority Leaders traditionally work their way up the leadership hierarchies, these "elections" are usually little more than an opportunity for the rank and file to deliver a series of speeches extolling the bold leadership of their respective party leaders. Anyone looking for excitement must wait for the periodic leadership fights inside the party caucuses.

The House Minority Leader designates two members for appointment to House Ways and Means and one member for every other House committee, including the House side of joint committees. (More on the composition of committees later in this chapter and in Chapter 4.) The Speaker must appoint the Minority Leader's designees to committees. The Speaker may appoint other Republicans as well, and often does. For example, there are four Republicans on House Ways and Means and two on most other committees (except the Committee on Bills in the Third Reading, which has only one).

The Senate has no such requirement, but, by custom, the President follows the Minority Leader's suggestions for appointment of Republican members to committees.

Majority and Minority Leaders. When members reach the Assistant Majority Leader level, they are potential successors to the Speaker or the President. This makes them powerful. Other members try to stay in their good graces, because someday all the committee appointments may rest in their hands. But this power does not give them license to do whatever they please. Members in leadership positions tend to become cautious in dealing with the Speaker or President in order to maintain their own positions.

There are occasional exceptions in the usual line of succession. Leaders may fall out of the good graces of the Speaker or President. A new Speaker or President may change the line of succession set up by the previous one. Occasionally an honorary appointment to one of these positions is made in recognition of a person's seniority or service, but it is understood that the appointee is not seriously considered a possibility for further advancement.

Majority and Minority Leaders are supposed to do just that: lead the members of their respective parties. Usually the leadership is present at all working sessions. During debate on a controversial issue, the leaders walk around the floor, talking to members, taking preliminary vote counts for the Speaker or the President, and trying to sway a few more members to support the party's position. Traditionally, that job is reserved for the **whips,** who are actually the lobbyists for the leadership's positions on legislation.

Committees and Committee Chairs

Committees are the workhorses of the legislature. All bills have to pass through at least four committees before being finally enacted, and it is important to understand the particular role each of these committees plays in the process.

Because committee work is so important, the chairs of key committees are considered part of leadership. For instance, the joint committees of Human Services, Taxation, Housing and Urban Affairs, Health Care, and Ways and Means all deal with controversial public issues, so the chairs of these committees are likely to be part of the inner circle of leadership. Human nature dictates, as well, that other chairs who have close personal ties with the President or Speaker will exercise extra influence over the leadership's agenda.

The Joint Committees

Most bills are assigned to one of the 22 joint committees organized around specific issue areas. Each joint committee has 17 members, 6 senators and 11 representatives, including a house chair and vice chair, a senate chair and vice chair. Committee staff are assigned to the chairs, and work out of their offices.

Legislators request appointment to committees which will give them the most visibility and influence in their districts. For instance, a legislator from a rural area would covet an appointment to the Joint Committee on Natural Resources in order to attend to the affairs of the hunters and farmers in the district, while a legislator whose district contains a large urban population of minorities might request Human Services and Elderly Affairs.

Leadership is quite open about using the power to appoint members to coveted committees as reward or punishment, and legislators wage internal campaigns to demonstrate their loyalty and expertise in order to obtain—and, sometimes, even keep—an appointment to a key committee.

The chairs of joint committees are responsible for the substantive policy work done in the legislature. They must master the intricacies of any controversial issues before their committee, lead the floor debate for most committee bills, represent their branch in any negotiations with the administration or the other branch, and serve as the expert spokesperson with the press. For the most part the Senate and the House chairs of the joint committees work well together—at least in public. Clashes of personality and style are not uncommon, however, and will become apparent when the committee meets as a whole to debate hot issues.

The Standing Committees

Both the House and the Senate have standing committees of Ways and Means, Third Reading, Rules, and Ethics. The Senate has another standing committee of Steering and Policy. Standing committees function within each branch and have members only from that branch.

Ways and Means.　The Ways and Means committees in both branches are extremely important because both deal with all legislation affecting state finances, including the state budget. All of Chapter 7 is devoted to a discussion of Ways and Means.

Bills on Third Reading (BTR).　This committee is small in membership (three) but very large in clout, since their duty is to review all bills for technical accuracy before enactment. Almost as influential as the Chairs of Third Reading are the staff attorneys who actually do the painstaking work of combing through bills for drafting errors and punctuation mistakes. Since Supreme Court decisions have balanced on the difference between *may* and *shall*, wise lobbyists will try to flag problems by meeting with BTR staff before their bill gets to that committee. (See Chapters 4 and 5 for more on BTR.)

Rules.　Chaired by the Speaker in the House, and the President in the Senate, these committees are big in membership (11 in the Senate, 25 in the House) but do little except grant joint committee extensions for considering bills and approve resolutions congratulating local sports teams, beauty queens, and retiring local politicians. While members of the Rules Committee do not need to meet to perform these functions, they do convene from time to time to formally endorse changes in the rules of procedure for their branch. For the most part, decisions of the Rules Committee are made by the President and the Speaker acting alone, or with the advice and concurrence of a few trusted others. In return for their labors, the rest of the members of Rules are entitled to call themselves Assistant Majority Leaders.

Committee on Ethics. Nobody likes being in a position to judge the professional ethics of a peer, but both branches have an ethics committee which has performed that unhappy task when necessary.

Committee on Steering and Policy (Senate) Rules "reforms" passed in 1984 created a new standing committee in each branch called Steering and Policy. These committees were charged with different responsibilities in each branch. House Steering and Policy was supposed to work with the Speaker and the Clerk to coordinate the scheduling of Committee Hearings and the formal session in an attempt to avoid serious conflict—for instance, a controversial bill from the Health Care Committee appearing on the calendar on the same day as the regularly scheduled Health Care Committee hearings. After a valiant attempt to organize busy people with hectic schedules and very different definitions of "controversial," the House Committee was dissolved in 1986.

This particular rules reform in the Senate resulted in a new way to delay a bill. Any bill reported favorably from a Joint Committee or Ways and Means must go to Senate Steering and Policy, where it may not be amended but may be held for up to 45 days before being put on the calendar for second reading. Steering and Policy is not required to hold hearings or open meetings of its membership, which includes the Senate President, the Majority Leader, the Majority Whip, the Chairperson of Ways and Means, and the Chairperson of Third Reading.

Discharge Procedures. Standing committee discharge procedures involve slightly different rules in each branch that can be used by members to force standing committees to report out bills. Generally, a specific motion must be made, it must be printed on the calendar, and must be supported by at least a majority (sometimes two-thirds) of the members present and voting. Even members who have legitimate gripes with undemocratic chairpersons and whose bills have widespread support from the general membership rarely try to get their bill unstuck with a discharge motion, lest they be characterized by their colleagues as posturing fools attacking the integrity of the leadership. Historically most discharge motions come from members of the minority party attempting to embarrass the leadership. They are successful only when the leadership is very weak or very wrong.

Legislative Staff

Typically, constituents calling the state house to register their opinion are offended when they can't get through to their representative and have to talk with staff. At the other extreme, some super-efficient lobbyists cultivate relationships with competent staff, defining a good day as any in which there is no personal contact with an elected official. The correct posture is, of course, somewhere in the middle.

Legislative staff fall into the two general categories: personal aides and policy staff. The best advice for constituents and lobbyists alike is to go through staff to request a meeting with the legislator, using the request as an opportunity to brief the staff person on the specifics. Always follow up with staff after any meeting or conversation with a legislator; legislators promise action, staff make it happen. You may find yourself blocked by a stubborn or stupid staff person. There is nothing to do but try to get access to the legislator through other avenues, including colleagues and friends.

Personal Aides. These are the people assigned to handle personal requests of constituents, which range from obtaining state college applications to fixing a traffic ticket. Aides take the calls and read the letters supporting or opposing pending legislation. Usual office practice includes regular memos to the boss summarizing the daily requests and drafting a response.

Aides usually know a little about everything going on in the state house: the hot issues on the calendar, the current crisis in the district, the status of some pending bills, the opinions of the local newspapers, and the bosses' schedule for the day. Good aides are patient and polite to constituents and are as forthcoming as permitted. Good aides keep files by issue, write down names and telephone numbers, and can decipher the same from the notes the boss throws on their desk with a, "Here, take care of this guy, will you?"

Policy Staff. These people know more than you really wanted to know about whatever issue they are researching at the moment. Policy staff are usually assigned to joint committees and are responsible for developing an analysis of pending legislation for the chairperson and the members. Smart committee staff welcome good, accurate information from lobbyists and constituents (from almost anybody actually), and they are very agreeable about meetings. Sometimes policy staff develop such a high level of expertise and exert such an influence over the development of public policy that they survive a dozen changes in chairs and leadership.

What Makes Legislators Act?

Every legislator takes a number of factors into consideration when developing a position on an issue. The same factors will be given a

What makes legislators act.

different weight at a different time by the same legislator, depending on a hundred variables—including an unhappy marriage and indigestion. Following is the short list of the the most influential factors that are always taken into consideration by every legislator, no matter what.

The Legislator's Personal Goals

People who become state legislators usually work hard, spending a lot of time and money to win their positions. Why? For most of them, becoming a legislator fits in with one or more of their personal long-range goals. Some legislators see their positions as stepping stones to higher office—perhaps Governor or Congressperson. Others see it as an effective way to change social policy. Others enjoy the power, prestige, and sport of politics for its own sake. Most legislators share some combination of all these goals.

But a legislator's goals will be attained only if she or he achieves some short-run objectives:

- getting reelected;
- gaining influence within the legislature; and
- avoiding conflict with either the legislative leadership or with his/her constituents.

These objectives are related. It is easier to get reelected if you are powerful in the legislature, because your constituents will believe you can get things done for them. Conversely, electoral defeat will quickly abort your climb to the top of the legislative heap.

Most legislators' actions are practical responses to these three short-term goals: (1) getting reelected by pleasing constituents; (2) gaining influence in the state house by pleasing the leadership; and (3) avoiding conflict on both ends. Let's look more closely at how these act and interact.

Getting Reelected.   Each legislator must judge which actions and reactions will most likely get him or her reelected. This depends somewhat on the political attitudes of the legislator's own district. Brookline voters, for example, are more liberal than Wellesley voters, so a Brookline legislator will probably take more liberal stands on certain issues.

In many districts, however, election campaigns are not based on traditionally conservative/liberal stands on issues. Instead, candidates may take positions which concur with a perceived "public mood"—for example, a trend in favor of fiscal restraint and law and order and against government programs and regulations. A public mood is a vaguely stated assumption of what voters want their lawmakers to do; it's based on stories in the press, public opinion polls, and letters and phone calls to candidates. Sometimes a candidate believes that the public mood favors a policy which he or she has opposed in the past; if so, he or she may soften his or her position to appeal to this new trend. But, while many candidates will appeal to these generalizations in their campaign speeches, they know that most legislative seats are actually won or lost because of substantial funding, good organization, and a large network of contacts, rather than on political philosophy.

Once elected, the advantages of running as an incumbent usually assure reelection unless the legislator makes a lot of enemies in his or her district by refusing to support constituents' requests for help. Therefore, most legislators avoid saying no to people directly and assist as many constituents as possible. There are a number of typical methods for doing this.

First, a legislator spends a great deal of time and resources responding to individual complaints and problems of constituents, trying to solve their problems case by case.

Second, a legislator often postpones making a commitment on a bill, while reassuring voters that he or she is seriously considering it. This provides more time to see if constituents will support or oppose the bill. Sometimes the bill never comes to a vote. Stalling long enough may get the legislator off the hook—without having to take a position and thereby offend someone.

Third, legislators are more likely to respond best to those who potentially can help or hurt them in the next election. One legislator has described this as a series of "circles of influence" around the legislator. Family and close friends of the legislator are most likely to have influence. Campaign contributors and workers come next. Voting constituents make up the third circle. Finally, they listen to lobbyists and special interest groups who influence voters in the district. Different legislators rank these influences in different orders of importance, but *whatever the order, their own voting constituents are always an important part of it.*

Gaining Influence Within the Legislature

Meanwhile, back at the State House, the legislator is trying to gain influence within the legislature. **Influence** means the power to affect the decision-making processes of the legislature. Some members work hard to attain leadership posts because they believe the world would be better off if *they* decide which bills pass and which die. Others just want to be able to deliver more state resources to their own districts. And others enjoy power for its own sake.

The Speaker and President appoint members to these posts and can strip these honors away. Because the Speaker and President often heed the advice of other leaders, rank-and-file legislators who want to move up the leadership ladder must stay in grace with them all. They do so by becoming good "team players." That is, they (1) become "experts" on a couple of issues and participate in debates relating to them; (2) attend sessions regularly; (3) and finally—but perhaps most importantly—always vote against any rules reforms which would diminish the leadership's power.

Legislators spend most of their time trying to keep everyone happy—both the leadership and their own constituents. If a con-

Avoiding conflict.

flict arises which forces them to choose between the desires of these two groups, they will lose either influence within the legislature or the goodwill of their voters. Naturally, they avoid getting into these sticky situations whenever possible. A common way to do this is to avoid being known as a liberal or a conservative. Most legislators call themselves "moderate," "middle-of-the-road," or "for the average guy." Such characterizations appeal to a broad audience and give the legislator the greatest amount of flexibility.

Theoretically, legislators could often be caught between the wishes of the leadership and those of their constituents. But a number of things prevent this in many cases. First, most people in the legislator's district have no idea what the legislator is doing at the State House. Except on the few public issue bills, the legislator can just go along with the leadership or with his or her friends.

Second, a legislator may never have to take a public stand on an issue. Most bills are passed or rejected on voice votes in which the reps and senators just say "aye" or "no" as a group; then the presiding officer of the session determines the result based on what he or she hears. (See Chapter 5 for more on voting procedure.) On these bills, the members' names will never be recorded with their votes, so neither their constituents nor the leadership will know how they voted.

Third, the leadership does not care about every bill. Even a bill forced to a roll call vote may not be a major issue for leadership.

Fourth, when a bill has attracted a lot of public attention and a member's constituents are clamoring for him or her to vote a certain way, the leadership will sometimes forgive a member for voting against them. The leadership understands the problem of strong constituent pressure. If a member has already taken a public position on an issue and voting with the leadership could embarrass the member and alienate his constituents, the leadership will probably overlook the vote.

Fifth, many constituent problems can be dealt with in non-legislative ways. For example, a member receiving a complaint about a defective car or an unfair eviction may call the salesperson or landlord to resolve the dispute rather than filing a bill to tighten protections for consumers or tenants.

Public Opinion

There are public moods on many issues, such as reducing property taxes, cutting welfare, and mandating tougher prison sentences. The legislator sometimes represents his constituents by going along with perceived public mood.

Public opinion, however, is general. It tells them to cut property taxes, but not *how* to do so. Should property taxes be replaced by more progressive taxes on richer taxpayers, thus maintaining revenue for public services? Or should welfare, police, fire, and school services be axed when property taxes are cut? How can legislators use public opinion to know how to vote on specific bills?

Legislators keep abreast of public opinion but take it with a grain of salt. They know that public opinion can be created or destroyed by media, pollsters, and interest groups running a good lobbying campaign. They listen to it only if they think it reflects the views of their own particular constituents. If perceived public opinion conflicts with the desires of the leadership or constituents, public opinion usually loses out.

The Legislator's Image

Legislators have certain images of themselves, and they often listen most closely to those with similar images. For instance, young urban Democrats might find a communality in their concerns for mass transportation, the needs of the poor and unemployed, and adequate fire and police protection. Suburban progressives—Democrat or Republican—might worry about legislative rules reform, long-term energy policy, and tax reform. Legislators from rural areas inevitably band together on issues protecting the environment and the integrity of local government. Some legislators view themselves simply as liberals, conservatives, or moderates. Some associate with special interests such as prison reform, aid to the handicapped, or women's rights. All of this informal bonding makes it easier for legislators to decide how to vote on a given issue. They just look at how their friends are voting—and follow suit.

Pressures on the Leadership

Leadership, like other legislators, must be reelected. Because it's particularly embarrassing for a party leader to lose a local election, leaders listen to their constituents very closely and use the power of their positions to accommodate constituent requests promptly.

In addition, the President and the Speaker must stand for re-election a second time—to their own leadership posts. And anyone who thinks that those votes are locked up because of past favors or appointments should be reminded of the oldest political comeback in the world, "What have you done for me lately?" In fact, every day is election day for the Speaker and the President. In order to hold onto their personal power and their role as the chief spokespersons for their respective branch, they must exercise real power and figure ways to get some decisions made within the legislative process.

The Speaker and the President cannot avoid conflict; they must confront it, resolve it, and sometimes take the blame for it. Since real power in the legislative process is defined as the ability to influence the outcome, both the President and the Speaker must take responsibility for an unpopular new law—unlike a rank-and-file legislator who can explain away his ineffectiveness or lack of real power by blaming the fast gavel of the tyrannical leadership.

The waiting rooms of both the Speaker and the President are always jammed with special interest groups or their lobbyists armed with persuasive facts and compelling arguments that their cause is just and their time is now. And while it is sometimes useful to arrange a courtesy meeting at the beginning of a campaign, especially if the whole issue is brand new to the legislature, don't waste any limited access you may have with either the President or the Speaker on a meeting just to say hello.

Any and all meetings, letters, or phone calls directed to the leadership should have one goal: Getting on the agenda for action. Leadership does not generate policy; it reacts to the proposals suggested, or demanded, by others. Most frequently those proposals come in the form of bills filed by members, who are in turn

Leadership must figure out how to get some decisions made within the legislative process.

responding to a constituent or special interest group. Your legislative campaign should create a public debate which the leadership is obligated to resolve—somehow.

To effect a resolution, the Speaker and the Senate President first must evaluate the strengths of often-conflicting positions on legislation from the Governor, other outside special interest groups, committee chairs, the informal regional and ideological caucuses, and (last but not least) one another. Then, they try to meld a majority coalition around the most acceptable solution—to pass the bill, to amend it, or to let it die. Because they don't have time to do this work on every bill, the leadership usually works hardest to develop a coalition on bills for which there is the greatest public clamor for a resolution. So, if you want your bill to be one of these, you must keep the heat on them.

Sometimes issues are debated and debated with no progress until both the problems and the debates have disappeared (sometimes dropped out of exasperation or exhaustion). If this is due to the leadership's inability to identify and build a majority coalition on one side of the question or the other, then the leadership has failed at its main function. If they fail on many issues, you may assess this leadership team as ineffective. As a lobbyist, it's important to determine whether the leadership is weak or strong in order to assess their help or hindrance for your bill.

How to Influence a Specific Legislator

Use Whatever Influence that Legislator Responds to

In the preceding pages, we identified some of the sources of pressure on legislators:

- the leadership;
- the affected constituents;
- constituents with connections to key legislators;
- information documenting the "public mood" (including media and polls); and
- facts and figures which outline the need, the cost, and the beauty of your proposed solutions.

Use whichever of these will most strongly sway the legislator you're working with. You may have to ask others with experience working with that member to give you some hints; talk to the legislator's staff aides or other friendly lobbyists. If you do a lot of lobbying, you will eventually know what approaches work best with each person.

Use Effective Communications

Written and oral communications with legislators have two purposes: (1) to obtain the legislator's support for your bill, and (2) to find out where the legislator stands on the bill. In all contacts you must be clear, concise, and informative about how your bill will solve the problem it addresses. When meeting with or writing to a legislator, always give fact sheets and other backup materials about the bill. (See Chapter 3 for more on writing backup material.)

Most legislators rank the following types of contact with constituents from the most to the least effective.

Personal Visits and Telephone Calls. Personal, face-to-face visits with legislators and their constituents are usually most effective. Visits give both sides an opportunity for questions and feedback. You can schedule appointments with legislators by calling their aides. Inviting them to attend a meeting of concerned citizens in their own districts is even better, because there you're on your own turf and not in the intimidating, confusing State House. This advantage tips the balance of power in your favor. But visiting at the member's office does give you a chance to know more about him or her by observing the member's personal appearance and the trappings of the office. Phone calls share many advantages of personal visits, but the phone is less personal and allows the legislator to cut you off. Also you miss all the cues of his or her language and the looks of the office.

Personal Letters.   Personal letters can be very effective if well written. They should look *not* like form letters but, instead, like "mom and pop" letters—that is, a genuine response to a particular feeling or problem the writer has. Genuine, however, does not mean rambling chicken-scratches. Make sure your letter includes the following information:

- a clear explanation of the problem as it affects you;
- the bill's title and number;
- a statement of the action you want from the member;
- a statement of your role (resident of district, registered voter in the district, voting supporter of the legislator in the last election, advocate for residents of the district);
- your signature (legible) and your address; and
- a request for the legislator's commitment to support the bill.

Form letters.   If there is no time or opportunity to write a personal letter, form letters are the next best thing. Though these have less impact individually than personal letters, a flood of them from people in the network gives the legislator the idea that many people out there care.

Petitions.   Most legislators feel that almost anyone will sign anything; thus a petition is not an effective tool. Petitions, however, do show legislators that many people in their districts (who may be registered to vote) support or oppose a particular bill.

All of these means are far more effective than you may think. On most issues, legislators hear little or nothing from their districts. Sometimes just two or three visits, phone calls, or letters look like a landslide to the legislator and may be enough to win his or her vote. Only the most controversial issues will generate more public reaction.

Getting a Legislator's Commitment

Asking a legislator for support is one thing; getting a commitment for it is something else. Although you may be reluctant to ask for a commitment in your first attempts, do try. But be prepared for a noncommittal response. Legislator's avoid stating their positions as long as possible to avoid angering both you and your opponents.

Instead, they'll try to appease you with, "Thank you for your interest. I appreciate your taking the time to make your views known to me. I want to reserve my decision for now. I want to look at all sides of the question before deciding. I assure you that I will give my most serious consideration to this issue."

You can accept this in the first contact. But at some point, you will have to count how many firm supporters you have; then it's time to press for a commitment.

Even professional lobbyists disagree on how to elicit this commitment. Some take a hardline: "We have to ask you to say yes or no right now." Others are friendlier: "I hope you can be with us." Different legislators respond to different approaches depending on their personalities, how much they know or care about the issue addressed by the bill, and the strength of the support and opposition in the district. Generally, legislators hate to make commitments on bills—at all. If they are unfamiliar with the issue and haven't yet heard from the opposition, they are likely to resist even harder. Don't fight them; just keep feeding them information about the bill and keep building up the local support for it.

Groups with long-term legislative agendas must tread very carefully in this area of commitment. Your working relationships with legislators must be able to survive a negative vote or two. Legislators frequently criticize special-interest groups for demanding support on 100 percent of the issues. This is an overstatement born out of defensiveness, to be sure; but, even when legislators won't commit their support, keep the lines of communication open for the next time you need their votes.

Sometimes a legislator trusts a lobbyist enough to cheerfully confide, "Listen, I'm in the tank on this one—nothing personal. I'll get'cha another time." Loosely translated, this means that this particular member has committed his or her vote against you on this issue, but will be available on another issue later on. The legislator made a simple deal; the leadership or your opposition gave him or her something (a commitment to support that member's "pet" bill, for example) in return for a commitment to vote against you. You don't have to know the specifics—nor should you want to. The trade's been made. Take comfort in the fact that the legislator felt bad enough about it to ackowledge a debt for the next time you ask—in *your* tank next time. Remember that *before* you get huffy.

Remember What You Can Offer Legislators

Work. Each year every legislator must deal with thousands of bills and reply to hundreds of constituent requests. Even with larger staffs than they had in the past, representatives and senators

A legislator in the tank.

often have crowded and diverse agendas. They and their staff members simply do not know about most bills coming before them, and they appreciate any backup work you can do for them on your bill and related bills. Your best bet for winning allies is to arm them with up-to-date information. Your goal is to be treated as another staff person—dependable and trustworthy on your issue.

Issues, Platforms, and Press.   Many legislators are looking for issues—in order to enhance their political appeal, to champion a cause they believe in, or both. All seek positive attention in the press. You may have a good issue to offer them. Find the legislators who care about your problem and make them public heroes by arranging a press conference in their districts or an invitation to address the local troops at a meeting of your network. (See Chapter 8 for more on using the media.)

Constituent Service.   Legislators might get requests for help from constituents regarding the problem you're working on. If your group can take care of some of these problems by providing technical information or referrals to other groups or agencies, let the legislator know.

Political Support. When affected constituents make political demands, legislators are inclined to yield because they want, or may desperately need, votes in the next election. Your potential political support as voters is a strong tool. Use it. But use it wisely. Sometimes groups threaten a legislator with voter opposition at the next election if he or she does not vote with them on their bill. Before making such threats, be sure you can deliver both votes and money to another candidate in the election. If you threaten but cannot follow through, you will gain not only a permanent enemy but also a reputation as a blowhard. Power at the polls is always stronger when untested.

Use Limited Resources Wisely

You have limited resources, so you have to use them where they will make the biggest impact. The two groups which won't change their opinions much are your staunch supporters and most dire opponents. So, don't waste time on people or tactics that will not influence the outcome of your bill. Though it's comforting to talk to traditional supporters, don't overdo it. Supply them with information and arguments that they can use to sway others. Then move on to the "undecideds."

Don't spend much time on clear opponents either—*unless* it may result in a compromise which neutralizes their opposition. And don't dally too long eliciting support from those who have no clear interest in your issue. Just make sure they will not oppose your bill.

Thank People Who Come Through for You

Make legislators happy they supported you. A little thanks goes a long way. Legislators get lots of criticism and very little appreciation. Be the exception; they will remember it next time you ask for their help.

Short personal notes from the State House lobbyist and from local constituents after key meetings, votes, or procedural victories carry enormous weight. They show the legislator you're watching him or her carefully, keeping abreast of developments, and communicating with your network. The debate on stopping condominiums took six weeks in the Massachusetts Senate in 1981. There were only eight key votes during that time, but the lobbyist and the tenants systematically thanked each senator who stuck with them.

Before it was over, those senators and their staffs were thoroughly invested in the issue and began to look forward to getting their daily instructions before going into the chamber to vote. That shows the power of thanking people to build a sense of commitment and willingness to put their full weight behind your issue.

Chapter 3

DRAFTING AND FILING THE BILL

The Four W's of Filing

When?

In Massachusetts the deadline for filing bills is 5:00 p.m. on the first Wednesday in December in even-numbered years and the first Wednesday in November in odd-numbered years for the session beginning the following January. If you miss the deadline, a bill can be **"late filed."** But late files must be approved by the House and Senate Committees on Rules, and then by 4/5 of the members of each branch. Usually only leadership-approved bills get this approval, so *you must meet the deadline.*

Bills filed by state agencies have a different deadline: the first Wednesday in November. The Governor, and only the Governor, can file a bill at any time during the session.

Who?

Bills must be filed by a state legislator (unless filed by the Governor or a state agency). In Massachusetts, citizens have the **"right of free petition,"** which allows anyone to petition the legislature for a law on any subject, but these petitions must be signed by a legislator. Legislators, however, are obligated to file a bill for any constituent who asks.

Bills may be filed by House members, Senate members, or both.

To the Honorable Senate and House of Representatives of The Commonwealth of Massachusetts
in General Court assembled.

The undersigned, citizens of _____, respectfully
petition for the passage of the accompanying bill or resolve, and/or for legislation

①
AN ACT ESTABLISHING A PUBLIC GUARDIANSHIP COMMISSION

Petitioners are requested to sign names and addresses legibly. ③

②

[signatures]
Mary Jane Gibson
David Cohen
Paul C. Kollias
Barbara A. Hildt
Kevin P. Blanchette
James T. Brett

26th Middlesex
11th Middlesex
7th Worcester
1st Essex
16th Essex
14th Suffolk.

A Massachusetts House petition for the guardianship bill: (1) Print the full title, beginning with AN ACT in all caps; (2) get the signatures of sponsors; and (3) indicate the districts they represent.

What?

Petitions and Bills. A bill is filed in two parts, the petition and the bill. You can pick up petition forms and bill paper in the House and Senate Clerks' offices. House petitions are white, the Senate's blue.

The **petition** includes the title of the bill, the names of the legislative sponsor(s), and any other citizen or organization sponsoring the bill. The petition is filed with the **bill** itself. A bill is legislation in draft form. In drafting or writing a bill, the major rule is: *If only certain words or phrases of the existing law are to be struck out or inserted, strike out the whole sections or paragraphs where these appear and rewrite them completely in the desired final form.* Many bills filed each year violate this rule, but few are rejected for it. Corrections are made in committee or by House or Senate counsel later on in the process.

Remember that laws change continuously; the changes are recorded in updated additions to hardbound law books. Ask the lawyer assisting your group to make sure your bill amends the *most recent version* of the law.

Fact Sheets and Other Backup Documents. The next job is to prepare a fact sheet for your own use with legislators, the press, and your organization's membership. The fact sheet should include spaces for:

- the bill's number and title;
- the names of the bill's sponsors;
- the committee to which it will be referred;
- the actions taken on the bill by the committee or by either branch of the legislature; and
- the name of a contact person for more information.

Some of this information cannot be filled in at the start of the campaign; instead, you add information as the bill progresses through the legislative process.

In the body of the fact sheet, explain the problem existing under current law and show how your new law will solve this problem. Don't try to pack every little detail into the fact sheet. Restrain yourself to writing a one-page fact sheet. Shorter, simpler fact sheets are more likely to be read by legislators and their staffs.

Put all your juicy details in a separate **section-by-section summary** of the bill. One of the problems with legislation is that it's written in "legalese." A section-by-section summary simply translates each part of the bill into ordinary English.

Also, you may decide to prepare additional memos with more

The Commonwealth of Massachusetts

IN THE YEAR ONE THOUSAND NINE HUNDRED AND EIGHTY-NINE ①

AN ACT ESTABLISHING A PUBLIC GUARDIANSHIP COMMISSION ②

Be it enacted by the Senate and House of Representatives in General Court assembled, and by the authority of the same, as follows:

③ SECTION 1.   Chapter 10 of the General Laws, as appearing in the 1986 Official Edition, is hereby amended by inserting after section 35G ⑤ the following new Section:--

④ Section 35H.   There shall be established and set up on the books of the commonwealth a separate fund to be known as the Public Guardianship Commission Fund, to be used to meet the operational costs of the public guardianship commission established under the provisions of chapter two hundred and twenty one B, ⑥ in addition to any appropriation from the General Fund.   Said Fund shall consist of amounts received from public and private sources as gifts, grants, donations, bequests and devises of money and any amounts to be received by said commission in fees for services pursuant to section seven of chapter

NOTE. – Use ONE side of paper ONLY. DOUBLE SPACE. Insert additional leaves, if necessary.

The guardianship bill in draft form: (1) Type in the year the bill will be considered in caps after the hyphen; (2) type in all the remaining words of the title after the words AN ACT; (3) begin the text of the bill (additional pages can be attached on plain white paper, double-spaced); (4) the section of the General Laws which the bill adds are typed in small letters and underlined; (5) statutory references are typed in numerical form; and (6) in the "General Laws" section, references to statutes are spelled out.

detailed facts, figures and analysis. These are especially helpful to the staff or to the few legislators who wish to become expert on this bill.

Where?

In Massachusetts, bills and petitions are filed in the office of either the House Clerk or the Senate Clerk. The House and Senate have slightly different customs about who can bring in bills and petitions. The Senate Clerk requires the legislative sponsor (or a staff member who has written authority to act for him or her) to hand-deliver these documents. The House Clerk, on the other hand, will usually accept them from anyone, if it has the required signatures.

Be sure to keep copies of all three documents. It will take some time before printed copies of the bill will be available. You will be doing some lobbying in the meantime, so you and your bill's sponsors should be well-stocked.

Strategic Considerations

So far it all sounds pretty mechanical. Draft it; type it; get it signed; bring it to the Clerk's office on time. Although these steps are routine, like everything else in a legislative campaign, there are underlying strategy considerations.

The Filing Deadline

You should always meet the filing deadline—especially if your bill may become controversial. Don't give the legislature an easy shot at refusing to consider it at the beginning. It's hard to get the support of 4/5 of the membership for permission to late file a bill. So, if many people will be collaborating on drafting the bill, begin on it in September at the latest.

Drafting

The major strategic question in drafting the bill is how broad or narrow the language should be. Rarely does a bill pass in its original form. The legislative process is full of opportunities for amendment and compromise. Usually you should draft the bill more broadly than necessary because its scope can be narrowed later. Also, add provisions which can be traded away later if compromises become necessary. Your group should make preliminary decisions on which

```
FACT SHEET
    S.663      H.1757

AN ACT ESTABLISHING A PUBLIC GUARDIANSHIP COMMISSION

Sponsors: Sen. Kraus, Padula, Cellucci, Barrett, J. Burke, and Webber
          Rep. Gibson, Cohen, Kollios, Hildt, Blanchette, and Brett


Hearing: Human Services & Elderly Affairs Committee , March 6th

    The Problem: Many elderly and disabled people are not competent to decide
where to live, what medications or medical care they need or how otherwise to
spend their money (which, in many cases, includes life savings of thousands of
dollars).  It may become necessary for a Probate Court to appoint a guardian or
conservator to make these decisions.  Unfortunately, many incompetent people
have no family or friends to act as guardian or conservator, and volunteers are
hard to find to take on this responsibility.  When no one is found, decisions
are not made, monies are not spent and, in some instances, services or benefits
are not provided, often with the result that the incompetent person must be
institutionalized.

    What This Bill Does:  This bill establishes an independent and autonomous
Public Guardianship Commission under the Supreme Judicial Court.  The Commission
(or a fiduciary non-profit organization with which it contracts) may be
appointed as guardian, guardian-ad-litem, conservator, trustee, representative
payee or monitor for an incompetent person for whom there is no one other than
the Commission or its contractee to serve in this capacity.  The bill does not
change the law as to when a fiduciary may be appointed, but only provides an
organization that is available to act in this capacity when necessary.  The bill
would go into effect as a pilot project serving those in need only in Bristol,
Essex and Suffolk Counties.

    The language of the bill makes it clear that the Commission will
encourage and support families and friends to serve as fiduciaries, with
assistance from the Commonwealth, if necessary; promote and support the
provision of fiduciary services by local, non-profit organizations in order to
establish a decentralized delivery system; provide extra safeguards for the
rights of wards and proposed wards; and thereby ensure that every person served
is provided with caring, high quality and individualized service.  Prior to
adopting a service delivery model, the Commission must solicit and take into
consideration the views of all interested persons.

    The Commission or its contractee may be appointed as a fiduciary only when
there is no less restrictive way of meeting the needs.  All decisions of the
fiduciary must reflect the individual character, desires and circumstances of
the incompetent person; and the incompetent person must be allowed to make his
or her own decisions to the extent possible.  The fiduciary may not be appointed
unless it first determines that it is able to provide high quality services.
The nine-member Commission includes an elderly person, a disabled person, an
elderly advocate, a disability advocate and an elderly or human service
provider.

    For More Information please contact Judith Lennett at Cambridge and
Somerville Legal Services (492-5520), Ernest Winsor at Mass. Law Reform Inst.
(742-9250) or Judy Meredith at Meredith at Meredith & Associates (262-3285).

12/15/88
```

A fact sheet for the guardianship bill.

provisions of the bill are essential and which can be watered down or dropped in the final version.

But there are limits. If the bill is drafted too broadly and extremely, no one will take it seriously. Bills which plan for the complete reorganization of the Secretariat of Human Services or which abolish the property tax system are definitely too broad.

Also, some bills are redrafts of unsuccessful legislation filed in

SECTION-BY-SECTION SUMMARY

AN ACT ESTABLISHING A PUBLIC GUARDIANSHIP COMMISSION

SECTION 1 establishes (in General Laws chapter 10, by a new §35H) the Public Guardianship Commission Fund as a segregable fund in the public fisc. The section was an insertion made by Senate Ways and Means in 1987.

SECTION 2 amends General Laws, chapter 201 (the general guardianship statute), section 6 to add the Public Guardianship Commission (and any agency contracting with it for guardianship services) to the existing list of persons and organizations which may petition for and be appointed as guardian of a mentally ill person.

SECTION 3 makes similar accommodating changes in §6A of c. 201, relating to mentally retarded wards.

SECTION 4 makes further accommodating changes, in §7 of c. 201, relating to court procedure after a guardianship petition is filed.

SECTION 5 makes accommodating changes in §14 of c. 201, relating to temporary guardianships.

SECTION 6 makes similar changes in the conservatorship section, §16 of c. 201.

SECTION 7 makes similar changes in §16B, relating to mentally retarded persons.

SECTION 8 makes changes in the temporary conservator section, §21.

SECTION 9 establishes a Public Guardianship Commission under the general superintendence of the state Supreme Judicial Court. This is the major section of the bill. There follow specific summaries of the sections of the new Chapter 221D of the General Laws which would be inserted by this SECTION 9.

Section 1 of the new Chapter 221D sets up the Commission, with nine members, six of whom represent special constituencies of elderly, disabled, providers and the chief judge of the Probate Court. Requires annual reporting to SJC and the legislature and an annual priority-setting process, mandating decentralized delivery

A section-by-section analysis for the guardianship bill.

past sessions; previous agreements with sponsors and supporters should be honored in the language of your new draft, unless all parties agree to start from scratch in the new session.

On the other hand, bills drafted too narrowly cannot be broadened later because the legislature's rules prohibit amendments or substitutions "**beyond the scope**" of the original bill. To keep open

HOUSE . . . . No. 1757

By Ms. Gibson of Belmont, petition of Mary Jane Gibson, David B. Cohen, Paul Kollios, Barbara Hildt, Kevin P. Blanchette and James T. Brett for legislation to establish a public guardianship commission. Human Services and Elderly Affairs.

The Commonwealth of Massachusetts

In the Year One Thousand Nine Hundred and Eighty-Nine.

AN ACT ESTABLISHING A PUBLIC GUARDIANSHIP COMMISSION.

Be it enacted by the Senate and House of Representatives in General Court assembled, and by the authority of the same, as follows:

1   SECTION 1. Chapter 10 of the General Laws, as appearing in
2 the 1986 Official Edition, is hereby amended by inserting after
3 section 35G the following new Section: —
4   Section 35H. There shall be established and set up on the books
5 of the commonwealth a separate fund to be known as the Public
6 Guardianship Commission Fund, to be used to meet the oper-
7 ational costs of the public guardianship commission established
8 under the provisions of chapter two hundred and twenty-one D,
9 in addition to any appropriation from the General Fund. Said
10 Fund shall consist of amounts received from public and private
11 sources as gifts, grants, donations, bequests and devises of money
12 and any amounts to be received by said commission in fees for
13 services pursuant to section seven of chapter two hundred and
14 twenty-one D.
15   All revenues created under this section shall remain in said
16 Public Guardianship Commission Fund, subject to appropri-
17 ation, to meet the operational costs of said commission. All
18 monies, as determined by the comptroller, remaining in the Public
19 Guardianship Commission Fund, in excess of appropriations
20 from the Fund for the fiscal year then ending, shall on June
21 thirtieth of each year be transferred by the treasurer to the General
22 Fund unless the general court otherwise provides.

The guardianship bill as printed.

your option to add broadening language to your bill, give it a broadly stated title and make sure all relevant subjects are addressed in the original bill. For example, if you wanted to create lower electric rates by developing a new rate package and your bill's title referred only to electricity rates, a later amendment to include gas rates would be ruled out of order because it was beyond the scope of the original bill. It would be wiser to use the words "public utilities" in the title if you think that it might be broadened later. Our favorite example is a proposed amendment to include cats in a dog pooper-scooper bill. The ordinarily sedate and judicious clerk could not resist making a preliminary ruling to the presiding officer that the cat amendment was clearly outside the scoop of the original bill.

Titles

Bill titles often determine which committee will consider the bill. Some bills are straightforward, and there's no question about which committee they'll go to. Others involve more than one topic and could be sent to various committees. In these cases, give the bill a title which will send it to the committee most likely to return a favorable report. (See Chapter 4 on committees.)

Give your bill a non-controversial title. The title will appear in the legislative calendar whenever the bill is ready for floor action. Make the title appealing, but don't put in anything which will attract undue attention. On the other hand, legislators get irritated if the title is misleading—especially if, as a result, the bill passes! Keep your credibility by being clear without being sensational.

Sponsors

Qualifications of a Good Sponsor

When your bill is printed, your sponsors' names are listed at the top, and from that time forward your bill will be identified as theirs. Your sponsors' willingness to use their political clout will be critical to the success of your lobbying campaign. Your sponsors will serve as your advocates with their colleagues, as spokespersons with the press, and as negotiators with the opposition. They are the ones who can talk to the Chairperson of Ways and Means and find out what she's really thinking. They are the ones who can ask the Chair of Third Reading to put the bill on the top of the "do next" pile. Look for the following characteristics in potential sponsors.

Knowledge of the Subject. Choose someone who has worked on the problem the bill addresses. He or she will understand the issues and will be regarded as somewhat of an in-house expert by other legislators.

Key Positions. Select someone who is respected by other legislators. Most legislators will vote for or against a bill based on who

sponsors it. Sometimes you will have to get a more moderate legislator to sponsor your bill; consequently, you may have to draft it
more moderately. Though this seems undesirable, sometimes it's
the only way to get the bill passed at all.

Try to enlist sponsors who hold key positions, such as:

- members of the committee to which the bill will be steered;
- the committee chairs or vice-chairs;
- members of the Committees on Ways and Means if the bill will
  go there (see Chapter 7 for discussion of which bills go to Ways
  and Means);
- members of the Committees on Bills in the Third Reading;
- the assistant majority whips, the majority whip, the majority
  leader, the Speaker or President (although the general policy
  of a Speaker and President may be *not* to file legislation unless
  it relates only to their individual districts);
- people who have particular influence with any of the above;
- leaders of informal issue caucuses;
- a friend of the Governor; and
- legislators who cooperate with other sponsors and with your
  group.

Belief in the Bill.   It is extremely important to get sponsors who
really support the bill. A sponsor who decides later that the bill is
bad or embarrassing is the worst kind of sponsor, regardless of his
or her leadership position. Such sponsors will just "kill" the bill
quietly by letting others know their feelings. So, make sure your
sponsors understand what they are signing.

Seldom does anyone push a bill over the sponsor's objections.
Some sponsors file bills for constituents even though they oppose
the content of the bill. In these cases, **"filed by request"** is written
on the bill—tantamount to ordering a coffin for the bill.

Short of this, many legislators sponsor anything in the hectic
days just before the filing deadline just to keep constituents happy.
Often they put their names to bills which they don't understand
and they have little or no intention of really pushing. Make sure
they understand what the bill does and who is likely to oppose it, so
that they don't change their minds and switch sides on you later.

Willingness to Work on the Bill.   Get someone who will actively work on the bill. Many sponsors sign bills but leave it to
others to push them through. While you want to recruit sponsors
on whom you can call to help move the bill at crucial times or for
their credibility, try to get at least one who will actively recruit
supporters throughout the campaign.

An informed committed sponsor willing to use clout.

Number of Supporters

The number of supporters you'll need depends upon the bill. Some bills will pass with only a committee chair as the sponsor. Others will need the support of several sponsors. If you expect the vote to be close, having several sponsors locks in votes later on, because sponsors will persuade buddies to vote with them. Even if a sponsor later regrets signing onto a bill, he or she will seldom repudiate the bill publicly by voting against it.

But, as a general rule unless you know that there will be a close roll call vote at the end, it is better to undersponsor than to oversponsor. First, only the first six names will be printed. Second, why talk to thirty-five people to agree on amendments and strategy when you could talk to just three?

How to Recruit Informed, Committed Sponsors

Since a legislator files 60 to 100 bills each year, he or she can't plug hard for each one. Instead, legislators choose certain bills to be their top priorities for the season. Potential sponsors for your bill must consider it one of their own personal priorities.

To promote the importance of your bill, send copies of the fact sheets and the bill to potential sponsors a month before the filing date. Follow this up with two meetings with the legislator: (1) a thorough briefing by your group's lobbyist and (2) a meeting with local constituents. In this process, the legislator will begin to understand the problem your bill addresses, see the potential political power of the affected constituents, and identify the lobbyist as the official State House representative for your group.

These meetings are a good first step for an organization that has never lobbied before, because the results are usually very encouraging. Don't be afraid to ask a receptive member (one already identified as an ally) to sign onto your bill as a sponsor; most will be happy to do so. Frankly, most legislators would sign even a parking ticket if a delegation of local citizens asked them to. Meetings to hand over the bill and fact sheet can also be held in the district rather than at the State House. Then the lobbyist can get the legislator's signature on the petition later. If your group is not yet organized by district, send a statewide delegation to the State House for a day-long blitz of meetings with potential sponsors. (See Chapter 1, section on "lobby day.")

In addition to briefing the legislator about the bill, the lobbyist must also brief the legislator's staff. Again, starting early will help to build this critical relationship. Sometimes a good staff person will candidly warn a lobbyist not to "push the boss" to be the prime sponsor because he or she is not really in love with the bill. Back off. Better to have unenthusiastic supporters than unenthusiastic sponsors.

The legislator whose name appears at the top and on the outside cover of the petition is the prime sponsor. This name will be inextricably linked with the bill from now on. The prime sponsor is ex-

An ineffective sponsor.

pected to carry the bill through the whole process (unless he or she chooses not to) and will get partial credit or blame for the success or failure of the bill. This is a crucial choice and another reason to begin your recruitment process early.

The prime sponsor's signature belongs at the top of the list. Get this signature first or leave a space for it. Most legislators will respect an organization's choice in prime sponsors. Occasionally, a legislator will assertively insist on being the prime sponsor and will sign the petition at the top. Cross out the name and ask her/him to sign below—you won't get arrested.

Repeated Use of the Same Sponsors

Organizations involved in legislative campaigns every year may be tempted to use the same few friendly legislators as sponsors over and over. Though this is easier than breaking in new team members all the time, it's a mistake in the long run. Broadening organizational support within the legislature is just as important as broadening the organizational base out in the district. Enlisting new sponsors is one way to do it.

Chapter 4

COMMITTEES AND COMMITTEE MEETINGS

Committees make the first decisions on all bills. Their action will either give your infant bill a good start in life—or kill it. So, it's crucial to lobby committees effectively. This chapter describes how committees work and how you, the lobbyist, can affect the process.

Actually, your work begins even before the bill gets to a committee. First, you direct the bill to the committee where it will be most warmly received.

Getting Your Bill to the Right Committee

Which Committee Does What?

Bills are assigned to committees based on subject matter. Sounds simple, doesn't it? But like everything else in the legislature, there's always room for some pushing and tugging. Here's how it works in practice.

The House and Senate Clerks, with the approval of the House Speaker or Senate President, refer all bills filed by the December deadline to the appropriate committees.

Theoretically, if a bill's subject matter can be interpreted in several ways, it could go to more than one committee. The rules permit a single bill to be referred to two or even three committees, which could sit jointly to discuss it. But this seldom happens.

Usually, one committee stakes out a claim to a certain subject matter. Although there are no hard-and-fast rules for deciding which bills go to which committees, most bills go to the obvious ones—for example, welfare fraud bills go to Human Services, housing bills go to Urban Affairs. Bills addressing issues straddling more than one committee can sometimes be steered to the committee where a more favorable outcome is likely.

How to Steer a Bill

There are several ways to try to steer a bill. First, give the bill a title emphasizing a subject the desired committee handles. Second, try to get the chair of the preferred committee, or some committee members, to sponsor the bill. Third, persuade the chair of the desired committee to ask the Clerks or Speaker or President to steer the bill to that committee.

Discharge

Even if a bill's already been sent to a committee, it doesn't necessarily stay there. The committee can ask to be discharged from consideration of the bill, recommending the bill to a more appropriate committee. Usually, the chair of one of the committees involved requests this. Technically, Senate and House approval are required. Actually the transfer is negotiated among the chairs or staff, and their recommendation is almost always adopted. Of course you need everybody's cooperation to pull this off, but sponsors can usually get this courtesy extended to them unless the request is totally inappropriate.

The Importance of the Hearing

How important is the hearing for the bill's ultimate fate? Legislative insiders often play down the importance of hearings, while less experienced outsiders tend to overestimate their importance. A "good hearing" is one that educates the committee members about your bill, convinces them that your problem is serious and that your solution is both reasonable and workable. Testimony should be short and informative. Members of the organization should be encouraged to attend the hearing as witnesses and to spend another half-hour visiting with their own representative and senator and possibly tracking down their hometown newspapers' reporters to get some local press coverage. (See Chapter 8 on media strategy.)

Take advantage of committee hearing day. You have a chance to educate the public—including legislators not on the committee— about the problems faced by your special interest group. Legislators will be making decisions in committee and on the floor on many bills affecting the interests of your group members. The more they understand about each issue, the more they'll understand the big picture as your group sees it. Give the hearing a reasonable amount of attention. Your precise strategy will vary, of course, from bill to bill. For bills concerning public issues, you would probably try to create a big display to attract media attention (see Chapter 8, Using the Media). For nonpublic issues, you may choose to work more quietly.

Getting Ready for a Committee Hearing

The usual practice for most committees is to group bills by subject area, assign them to policy staff for analysis, and set tentative hearing dates. For instance, the Health Care Committee might assign all bills related to hospital administration to one staff person and bills related to drug and alcohol abuse to another, and then schedule hearing days based on the staff's estimate of time needed to complete the analysis. Of course some committees schedule hearings when bills are received from the clerk's office. In both cases, wise lobbyists stay in touch with the committee staff during the early weeks of the session to pick up advance information.

Many committees are willing to share, in advance, the entire list of bills to be heard on a given day, allowing experienced lobbyists to try and guess the exact time their bills will be heard. (They can guess all they want, but they're never right.) The "Daily List," available in the document room, publishes the list of bills being heard that day by any joint or standing committee.

Who Do You Talk To?

Talk to the people who have the most decision-making power or the most influence on those who do. This varies from committee to committee. All committees operate differently. Some are very democratic, while others are dominated by one chair or the other. In some, the staff have lots of influence; in others, they don't. Within a single committee, decision-making procedure may vary on different issues.

At this point you may be thinking, "This doesn't help at all. I still don't know who to talk to about *my* bill. This is one of the cases in which there is no substitute for experience. Lacking experience, talk to those who have it—people who have worked with this particular committee. Here are suggestions which would apply in most situations.

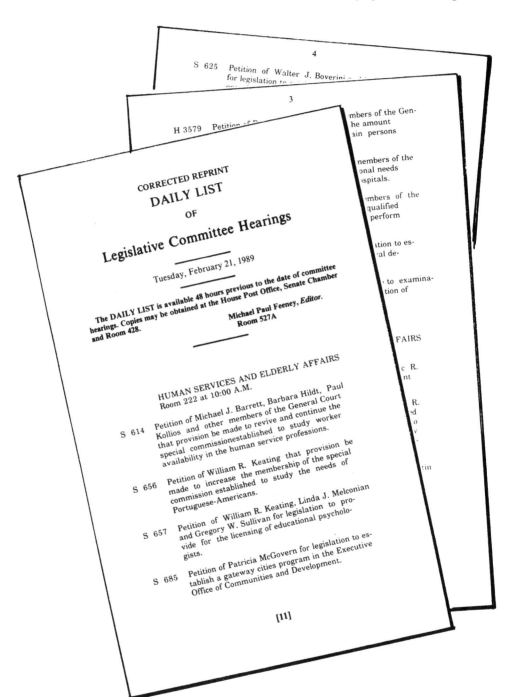

S 625   Petition of Walter J. Boverini
        for legislation to

H 3579   Petition of

CORRECTED REPRINT
DAILY LIST
OF
Legislative Committee Hearings

Tuesday, February 21, 1989

The DAILY LIST is available 48 hours previous to the date of committee hearings. Copies may be obtained at the House Post Office, Senate Chamber and Room 428.

Michael Paul Feeney, *Editor.*
Room 527A

HUMAN SERVICES AND ELDERLY AFFAIRS
Room 222 at 10:00 A.M.

S 614   Petition of Michael J. Barrett, Barbara Hildt, Paul Kollios and other members of the General Court that provision be made to revive and continue the special commissionestablished to study worker availability in the human service professions.

S 656   Petition of William R. Keating that provision be made to increase the membership of the special commission established to study the needs of Portuguese-Americans.

S 657   Petition of William R. Keating, Linda J. Melconian and Gregory W. Sullivan for legislation to provide for the licensing of educational psychologists.

S 685   Petition of Patricia McGovern for legislation to establish a gateway cities program in the Executive Office of Communities and Development.

[11]

The "Daily List" publishes the list of bills being heard.

See Both Chairs. Whatever the committee's power structure, both chairs will probably have a great deal to say about the fate of your bill. One of the worst mistakes is to deal with only one chair. In exceptional cases this may work, but try to "sell" your bill to each one. The Senate chair can do very little to promote your bill in the House, and vice versa.

The relationship between the two chairs is one of the most important in the legislature. The Senate chair officially presides over the committee, yet the House chair may have equal or greater power in the committee for a number of reasons. First, there are more House members on joint committees, so the House chair potentially controls more votes. Second, the Senate chair usually must rely on the House chair to carry legislation through the House. Third, House members are usually more active participants than senators at hearings and voting meetings.

In fact, either chair may dominate because of a stronger personality, better understanding of the subject, better staff, more power within his or her own branch, or more friends and respect in the other branch.

Often there is rivalry—occasionally bitter—between chairs based on historical and personal factors. Rivalry between the House and Senate is strong and long-standing; each chair has been appointed to uphold the policies and honor of the respective branch. Also, the attitudes of the House and Senate membership may differ on various issues. And the chairs may differ in their approach to programs and to committee procedure. Their personalities and styles may differ also.

In dealing with the chairs, know how they get along with each other. You have to deal with both without making an enemy of either one.

See Committee Members. You may not have time to see all members, but you should see enough to assure that:

- members inclined to support the bill are solidly behind it;
- uncommitted members understand the bill and their questions, concerns, and objections have been raised; and
- opponents' objections are clear.

Local constituents should be encouraged to join the lobbyist at these meetings with the committee members. In meeting with members, remember which forces affect their decisions. Besides wanting to hear about the bill and how many constituents in *their* district will be helped, committee members will want to know the opinions of the chairs and other committee members. Always tell the truth.

One goal of these pre-meetings is to help the committee members to *understand* the bill, thus preventing (hopefully) any confused questions or misleading statements at the hearing itself. Another goal is to build grassroots support among the committee membership itself to turn out a favorable report. Finally, you are building your list of supporters and opponents. When you identify supporters, encourage them to ask good questions at the hearing and remind them of the hearing dates. When you discover opponents, try to convince them to be passive if your case and its presentation are compelling. (You should not remind opponents of the hearing day or the executive session. What they don't know won't hurt you.)

While these meetings are going on in the State House, local constituents of the committee members should be calling or writing to their legislators to give the bill a favorable report.

Don't be discouraged if all these visits, calls, and letters do not result in instant commitments to support your bill. You won't know for sure until the day of the committee vote.

Talk to Staff.   In most committees, staff play a very important role in the committee's decisions. The chair listens closely to the advice of some staff people. In addition, the staff write reports on each bill. Though not every staffer directly influences the views of the committee chairs, they can indirectly affect these views by writing reports which either support or undercut a bill under consideration. The committee uses these reports in executive session to decide how to vote. At the very least, try to prevent staff from saying bad or incorrect things about your bill. Convincing them may go a long way toward convincing the committee.

Give the staff detailed analysis and background information on the bill. The staff has to summarize scores of bills, so any good information you feed them will probably appear in the bill's summary or analysis. Be sure your statements (especially facts and figures) are honest and accurate. If you mislead a staff person who is later caught by the chair or a member with incorrect information, that staffer will probably never trust you again—and will let others know about it, too.

Staff can also indicate who are your probable supporters and opponents on the committee. They may be especially informative about the feelings of the chair and can help you set up meetings with him/her.

Opponents.   When planning your legislative campaign, you assessed your opposition. If you know a group will oppose your bill at the hearing, try to find out how many of them will testify and what their arguments will be. This knowledge enables you to counter their arguments in pre-meetings with legislators and staff, and will also help you plan the type of testimony to present at the hearing.

Allies. You may want a big turnout and dozens of witnesses to testify; you may want to bombard the committee members with letters of support from different organizations; you may need only a few discreet visits from key supporters. Whatever your strategy, your allies need advance warning.

Hearing Strategy

What Kind of Testimony? Based on what you've learned from contact with committee staff and members, assess which kind of information will be most helpful. Usually a mix of the following kinds of testimony is best.

- *Technical explanations of what the bill does:* This is usually done by "expert" witnesses—that is, lawyers, doctors, economists, social workers, or others with technical expertise in your field.
- *Personal stories of the problem the bill seeks to solve:* This is best done by people who suffer under the current law—that is, the affected constituency. A personal story will usually be much more compelling than an expert's testimony. Second best is the testimony of advocates who tell stories about their clients' difficulties under the current law.
- *Political support:* Sponsors of the bill, other legislators, other elected or appointed officials, and supportive interest groups should testify in support of your bill.

Sometimes you would not plan to present all these kinds of testimony. For example, to convince a committee that a bill makes only technical changes in a current law, ten witnesses may make the members suspect that the bill is more controversial than it looks. In this case, one or two well-chosen witnesses might be better.

Written Statements

Just before or after testifying, submit a written statement to the committee stating your position and reasons for that position.

Testifying

Testifying is just like speaking at any public meeting. Begin with a simple:

Massachusetts Law Reform Institute
2 Park Square
Boston, Massachusetts 02116
Area Code 617
482-0890

Committee on Governmental Regulations
State House, Boston

    My name is Charles Harak and I am a lawyer specializing in
energy issues at Massachusetts Law Reform Institute.

    It is predicted that heating prices will increase another
27% next winter. President Reagan has recommended that federal
funding for fuel assistance be cut by 25% next year. The
President's cut in the program combined with a change in the
allocation formula could result in Massachusetts losing 45% of
its federal fuel assistance money. The severity of New England
winters, the unpredictability of oil supplies and prices in
Massachusetts, and the relative age and dilapidation of our
housing stock all combine to create a unique regional heating
problem. President Reagan has made it clear that his
administration, with the support of several governors, including
our own, will require the states to respond to these local
problems rather than looking to the federal government for
increased aid. It is therefore imperative that the legislature
move to put a program in place to address these problems.

    The bill creating a permanent state fuel assistance program
(S.717) which is before you will ease the impact of these
drastic cuts and escalating prices on the working poor,
low-income and elderly residents of the Commonwealth. By
setting an income eligibility level of 200% of CSA poverty
guidelines, the bill creates a program which is able to serve
those low-income working families and small elderly households,
who desperately need assistance but who are just over income for
the federal program. The bill also creates a weatherization
component to decrease recipients' dependance on assistance.

    I would like to leave you with a detailed section-by-
section analysis of the bill along with some other
documentation. If you have any questions, please contact me at
the above address. Thank you.

                                       Charles Harak
                                       Staff Attorney

Written testimony from an expert.

*"Good morning, Mr.(Ms.) Chairman(woman), members of the
committee. My name is_____. I am a lawyer speaking in support of
H.___." Or, "I am a welfare recipient from Worcester and I am speaking in support of H.___.*

Advocates and Experts.   Advocates or experts usually begin by
explaining the current law, what changes this bill will make, and
why the changes are needed. They mention examples of people
who would be helped by passage of the bill.

```
                                        February 23, 1989

Committee on Government Regulations
State House
Boston, MA

Members of the Committee:

     My name is John Pepino and I live at 2 Richfield Street in
West Newton.  I am here to testify in favor of S.717, An Act to
establish a permanent home heating assistance program.

     Last year my wife and I got $600 from the fuel assistance
program and ¼ I tell you ¼ we would have frozen to death without
it. Frankly, I wouldn't have known such a program existed if I
hadn't called Rep. DeNucci to tell him about our situation.
He's the only one who told me  who to call to get fuel
assistance.

     I think it should be a permanent program so people like my
wife and me can always be warm in the winter. I think if the
program was permanent, old people like me wouldn't worry so much.

     I hope you give this bill, S.717, a favorable report and I
hope you get it through the legislature this year.  Thank you.




                         John Pepino
                         2 Richfield Street
                         West Newton, MA
```

Written testimony from an ordinary citizen.

Number of Speakers.   Limit your number of speakers. Committee hearings last most of the day. Many bills are discussed and many people speak. The committee may set a time limit on each bill or on each speaker's time. It is important to show committee members that many people need and support the bill, but repetitious testimony may be irritating. Make the point, instead, by having lots of people contact the committee members before the hearing and by packing the hearing room with supporters who will also submit written testimony to the committee.

Residency of Speakers.   You should try to find witnesses who live in the districts represented by committee members. Legislators pay closer attention when one of their own voting constituents tells a real story about a problem happening right in the legislator's district. (As the old song from the *Music Man* says, "Yes, folks, we got trouble. Right here in River City.")

Media.   This is an ideal time to recruit friendly media to cover your story if this is part of your campaign plan. (See Chapter 8 on using media.)

At the Hearing

What to Expect

Newcomers to the State House expecting high drama at the committee hearing are often disappointed. Sometimes they must testify to a lone committee member. Even if several members show up, they may not ask a single question. Some members may be hostile to your issue and to your network for personal reasons. Some take phone calls during hearings. Other members walk out right during testimony. Or they may enter in the middle of a moving story and talk to each other while witnesses are speaking.

Suppress your desire to stand up and scream, "You are rude and boorish! I pay taxes to have you listen to speakers, not to be whispering and talking on the phone." This may be true, but it will not help your bill.

Whatever happens, remain calm. Respond to every question—even rhetorical or critical ones—with an answer detailing the need for your bill. Even though this may not win over blatantly hostile members, the undecided ones may be impressed with your conduct, demeanor, and quality of answers. Also, a legislator opposing you on this bill may become an ally on another, if you don't alienate him or her with tactless retorts.

A witness who is directly affected by the bill should tell the committee what life is like under the current law, what the bill would do, and how these changes would affect his or her life—the more personal, the better. Witnesses usually finish by offering to answer questions.

Procedures at a Hearing

Length of a Hearing.   It is nearly impossible to predict how long a hearing will last or at what point in the hearing your bill will be heard. The most predictable thing about a hearing is its starting time. *Be there promptly.* If witnesses are not there at the start, the chair may end the hearing immediately.

Order of Testimony.   The order in which bills are heard and witnesses called varies from committee to committee. Some committees take bills in numerical order, then ask all supporters to speak first and opponents second. They will not arrange the speakers in any particular order, so you must jump up there when you can. Some committees group the bills for the day by subject matter and call the bills within each subject in numerical order. In a few committees, people sign up as they enter and testify in that order, regardless of what bill they plan to talk about.

Often legislators are allowed to testify on bills whenever they arrive. This can be very frustrating for people from public interest groups who are waiting their turns. Sometimes legislators will speak at length, perhaps about a bill having little or no statewide impact, while the crowd of witnesses attending on their own time are forced to wait.

The privilege exists because legislators often have to attend to many simultaneous obligations—bills being heard on the same day by different committees, floor action sessions, and so forth. The legislators fear that if they fail to appear for the hearing, constituents and other members might assume they don't care about the bill. So they are allowed to speak whenever they can make it. Several committee chairs no longer practice this custom because they think it unfair; others limit the length of testimony legislators can present at unscheduled times.

Sometimes this custom can be used to your own advantage. Ask a legislator to testify for your side at the beginning of the hearing; this is like waving a flag over your bill, attracting the committee's attention right from the start.

What to Do After the Hearing

After the hearing, visit your supportive committee members and ask for suggestions and continued help. Contact members who appeared undecided at the hearing, answer their questions, provide them with written information, and try to persuade them to vote for a favorable report. Constituents should contact supportive and undecided committee members at this point, urging them to support the bill. *But it is a waste of time to contact definite opponents of the bill.*

The Executive Session

The committee votes in an **executive session,** during which only committee staff and members discuss the bill. Unless a majority of the committee votes to close the meeting to the public, this session is open.

Sometimes the executive session on your bill will be held right after the hearing; sometimes it is postponed. But whenever it's held, *you are allowed to and should be there when the committee votes.* Your presence is important because: (1) it will influence the waivering committee members' votes; (2) the members may have more questions you can answer; (3) you must make sure supportive

Rounding up members of a committee for an executive session.

committee members are there to vote, and if not, round them up; and (4) members may discuss new problems with the bill and propose amendments.

Various Kinds of Committee Reports

When the committee votes on the bill, we say it is **reported out of committee.** The committee can take one of the following actions on each bill.

Report that the Bill Ought to Pass.   This is the same as a **favorable report.** The committee can recommend passage of the bill in its original form, with amendments, or in new draft.

Report that the Bill Ought Not to Pass.   This is called an **adverse report** and is usually accepted on the floor. (See Chapter 5 for more on floor action on adverse reports.)

Report One Bill on Another.   This happens when a committee does not want to give a bill an adverse report, but doesn't want to admit they're killing it. It simply attaches the bill's number, not the text, to another bill related in subject matter to which it does give a favorable report. This gets the attached bill out of the committee, but no further action will be taken on it. The bill is dead unless the leadership pulls some parliamentary tricks to get such a bill revived—but it rarely does.

Study Order.   Here, the committee recommends that the bill be studied during recess. This recommendation usually means that the bill dies because funding for the study is never provided. Occasionally, a study is seriously undertaken; it may be useful on a controversial and technical bill. Most often, however, this procedure is used to kill a bill quietly.

Send It to Judicial Council for Study. The committee recommends this for some bills that affect the courts. This usually kills the bill for at least one session because the Judicial Council, composed of the chief judges of the various courts or their designees, seldom recommends favorable actions on anything that significantly changes court procedure. Even a favorable recommendation will not come out until the following year. Unlike most legislative studies, the Council does make an analysis and report. You should try to prevent an unfavorable Council report because it can be used against the bill next session. Provide the Council with the same documentation and arguments for the bill as you did the committee. A favorable report from the Council may help the bill's future.

Committee Voting Procedures

Simple Majority Votes. Technically, the committees' decisions on all bills are made by a simple majority vote. In practice, however, only a handful of members present at the executive session will determine which hat your bill wears out of committee. Usually members do not attend all hearings or all executive sessions. If a member specifically requests that the whole committee vote, they will round up all the absent members before taking the vote. If poor attendance threatens to yield an unfavorable report on your bill but you know most of the committee supports it, by all means ask a supporter to request such a poll.

Dissensions. In addition to simple agreement or disagreement on bills, individual committee members may also **dissent**. This means they seriously oppose the bill. Or they can "**reserve their rights**"—that is, they take no position so they can decide later when the bill comes to the floor. Names of dissenters are recorded, but not the names of those who reserve their rights.

Try to prevent dissensions on your bill. The appearance of a particular member's name as a dissenter may flag it as a bill to be opposed on the floor by that member's allies. A dissension by a committee chair is an almost certain death knell when the bill hits the floor of that chairman's branch. *Preventing a dissension is the only reason to spend your valuable time lobbying committee members who definitely oppose your bill.*

Reporting Deadlines: Joint and Standing Committees

A joint committee (and only a joint committee) must report (take action) on all bills referred to it. If the bill was filed by the December deadline, the report must come out by the fourth Wednesday in April. If the committee takes no action by then, the bill automatically receives an unfavorable report. The same applies to late-filed bills referred to the committee prior to April 15th. Bills referred after that date must be acted upon within ten days or be given an automatic unfavorable report. This happens not only with late files, but also with bills that are recommitted or discharged from one committee to another after April 15th.

It is possible to extend a deadline for reporting on a bill. Technically, the extension must be approved by the Rules Committees of both branches acting concurrently. If either Committee on Rules denies the extension, then it requires a 4/5 vote of each branch. In practice, such extensions are obtained easily. But most chairs, fearful that extensions will make them look inefficient to the Speaker or Senate President, request them sparingly and reluctantly. Usually they request extensions only when a major bill needs serious work or study, or as a device to postpone dealing with a controversial issue.

There are different reporting deadlines for the standing committees in each branch. There is no deadline for reporting bills out of either House or Senate Ways and Means or out of the Senate Committee on Third Reading. Bills reported to the House Committee on Third Reading must be reported out within 45 days, and most of them are reported out one way or another. Bills reported to the Senate Committee on Steering and Policy must be reported out within 45 days as well, and most of them are as well. In the case of both committees, bills that are recommitted for further study usually die with the end of the session.

From the Committee to the Floor

One committee member will be assigned to sign the committee's report. This member will be in charge of the report in his or her branch and is expected to lead the fight for this report during floor debate. Usually the chair will do this. If another member is assigned the task, it may indicate that the chair does not fully support the committee's action. Sometimes it is a move to get a less controversial person than the chair to carry the bill. Or it can be done as a courtesy to the committee member who filed the bill.

Once the bill is reported out of committee, the lobbyist starts preparing strategy for floor action. What happens on your bill on the floor and what you can do about it are the topics of the next chapter.

Chapter 5

FLOOR ACTION

View from the Gallery

From the Senate gallery you are watching the proceedings in the chamber below, waiting for them to get to your bill. If it passes, courts will be permitted to delay evictions which cause hardships for tenants. You've invested a lot of time on this bill—suggesting ways to draft it, getting your senator to sponsor it, and testifying at the Judiciary Committee hearing. Your hopes—and fears—are high.

On the Senate floor only about half of the senators are present. None seems to be paying attention to the proceedings. Your bill's sponsor, Senator Harold Traveler, is nowhere to be seen. Just this morning he assured you everything was set. He had talked to the Senate President and the chair of the Judiciary Committee, Senator Alfred Suzuki.

But Suzuki's not around either. In fact, neither is the Senate President. Instead, the Majority Leader is in the chair. Has Traveler talked to *him* about the bill? You're not sure.

After a long wait, the Majority Leader calls the number of your bill. "Calendar number 2199—third reading of the bill." The Clerk then reads the bill's title.

The Majority Leader says, "The question comes on passing the bill to be engrossed. The gentleman from Suffolk and Norfolk, Mr. Keyes."

Senator Keyes rises and says, "Mr. President, I move that the bill be laid upon the table."

The Majority Leader responds, "The gentleman from Suffolk and Norfolk, Mr. Keyes, moves that the matter be laid upon the table. Under the rules, postponed to next session."

View from the gallery.

"Oh, no!" you think. "I have to come back tomorrow."

Then Senator Keyes says, "Mr. President, I further move suspension of the rule so that the matter may be taken up forthwith."

"Mr. Keyes moves suspension of the rule so that the matter may be taken up forthwith. Is there objection? The chair hears none. The rule is suspended. The question now comes on laying the matter upon the table. All in favor, say aye; opposed, no. The ayes have it, and the matter is laid upon the table."

Senator Keyes continues, "Mr. President, I move reconsideration and I further move suspension of the rules so the matter may be taken up forthwith."

"The Senator moves reconsideration and further moves suspension of the rules so that the matter may be taken up forthwith. Is there objection? The rule is suspended. The question now comes on reconsideration. All those in favor, say aye; opposed, no. The nays have it and the matter is not reconsidered."

No one voted. No one debated. What happened?

Your bill got killed—that's what happened. Senator Keyes didn't like it and used the Senate rules in a perfectly appropriate manner to **table** it. According to Senate courtesy, a tabled bill can be removed from the table for debate and a vote only by the senator who originally made the motion to table. Senator Keyes also moved for reconsideration quickly to close any further debate on the issue.

So, unless you can convince Senator Keyes to remove your bill from the table (unlikely since he opposes it), there it will stay. And there it will die at the end of the session.

But if even one supportive member had been present and alert, he or she could have objected to the motion to suspend the rules or the motion to reconsider (or make the motion to reconsider themselves!), giving you time to round up supporters to defeat the tabling motion the next day.

When opponents are batting your bill around the floor, you may, in your frustration to do something about it, want to inject some helpful comments from the gallery. But this will only get you escorted out by a court officer.

But lobbyists can affect floor proceedings. Although you can't get down there and do it yourself, you can coach your supporters from the sidelines. To be an effective coach first you must understand how the game is played—its rules, its moves, its strategy. This chapter (1) describes these in detail and (2) shows how the lobbyist can use them to coach the floor team.

The Legislative Obstacle Course—or, the Three-Reading Process

Floor action refers to the formal meetings of the House or Senate to take action on bills reported out of committee. It bears little or no resemblance to descriptions of it in civics books.

Think of legislative procedure as an obstacle course with many hurdles each bill must scale. The committee report is one of the first. After the bill is reported out of committee, the route it takes depends largely on whether it got a favorable or an unfavorable committee report.

Adverse Reports

If a bill gets an adverse report, floor action consists of accepting or rejecting that report. The committee's adverse report goes to the branch where the bill originated (except adverse reports on money bills, which are always delivered back to the House). If that branch accepts the adverse report, the bill is killed. Sometimes a supporter on the floor, with leadership cooperation, can successfully "substitute" the original bill for the adverse report and can thereby resuscitate the bill, if only for a short time. But most adversely reported bills die.

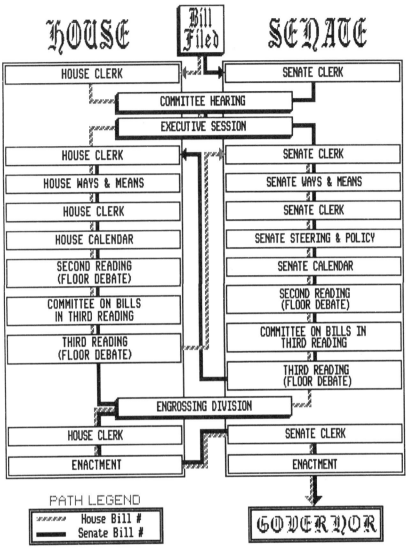

The three-reading process. House bills begin in the House; Senate bills begin in the Senate.

Favorable Reports—the Three-Reading Process

Before a bill is finally enacted (passed into law by the legislature), it must be "read" in each branch three times, ensuring members a fair chance to debate, delay, amend, or kill any piece of legislation. In practice, the first reading of a bill is the printing of the bill's number and title on the daily calendar. House bills generally go to the House Clerk and Senate bills generally go to the Senate Clerk to begin the three-reading process.

Printing on the Calendar. When the House Clerk receives a favorably reported bill from a committee, it is routinely scheduled for the next legislative day's calendar.

When the Senate Clerk receives a favorably reported bill from a committee, it is routinely reported to the Steering and Policy Committee for "scheduling." Most bills turn around quickly in Steering and Policy. Controversial bills might rest for a while at the request of a senator gathering support for floor debate. Steering and Policy must report a bill out after 45 days.

In both branches, bills receiving unfavorable reports from a joint committee are sometimes allowed to pile up in the clerk's office for a week or two and are printed on the calendar during a slow period. Bills affecting state finances go directly to House or Senate Ways and Means.

Calendars are printed every day the legislature is in session, unless in a previous session either branch specifically ordered that no calendar be printed. Calendars can be picked up in the Documents Room on the day of the session.

Second Reading—Debate and Amendment. Traditionally, the second reading is the time for extended debate and amendments on controversial bills. The Clerk reads the title of the bill aloud from the podium and the Speaker asks for a vote on ordering it to a third reading.

At this point, members may propose amendments to the bill, which are voted on before the vote is taken on the original bill. If the amendments pass, the bill is voted on as amended; if they fail, it is voted on in its original form.

Bills which pass the second reading vote are ordered to a third reading. Bills which fail are rejected and cannot be considered again during that session unless there is a motion to reconsider the vote. (See this chapter, section on "Deliberations" for more on reconsideration.)

If the bill is ordered to a third reading, the title continues to appear on the calendar. But the bill won't actually be read a third time until it has been approved by the Committee on Bills in the Third Reading (BTR), the next hurdle in the game.

Review by Committee on Bills in the Third Reading (BTR). This committee functions as the legal experts for the legislature. Technically they review all bills to make sure they are properly drafted and are constitutional. Traditionally, the membership of the committee is small (three or four legislators), and most of the responsibility falls on the chair. Since BTR can "report a bill out" in two minutes, hold for 45 days (House), or hold for eternal study (Senate), the Speaker and the Senate President always choose one of their most loyal members to chair this committee.

The actual work of reviewing legislation is done by one of the most professional and knowledgeable staffs in the State House. The staff is expected to reflect the chair's loyalty to the leadership. However, their legal expertise is so critical to the integrity of the legislative process that even the Speaker and Senate President have to ask twice to unglue their own pet bills from BTR if the staff has serious reservations about their constitutionality.

Bills get stuck in the BTR for several reasons. Occasionally, BTR decides that the bill has technical or legal flaws. If defects can be corrected without changing the bill's intent, the committee recommends that the bill be amended with the corrections or that it be replaced by a correctly drawn bill. These reports are almost always accepted on the floor.

Sometimes the committee staff just has a big backlog of work. Sometimes they don't understand the purpose of the bill, or it has a relatively low priority for them. Often legislators or lobbyists ask them to hold bills, and they will—unless, of course, a more powerful person wants the bill moved. Occasionally, a committee staff-person or a member of BTR may hold a bill simply because she or he does not like it.

Sometimes BTR asks to be **discharged** from further consideration of a bill. This report tells the members that the bill has problems which cannot be corrected without changing its meaning. The discharge report is almost always accepted on the floor, and the bill is likely to be rejected without strong public or political support to save it.

The discharge report has other uses. If the leadership, members, or lobbyists are pressuring BTR to move a bill out, BTR sometimes discharges it. This allows them to acquiesce to the request without approving the result. BTR will often discharge bushels of bills during prorogation, knowing that most of them are doomed to die before the session ends anyway. (See more explanation in this chapter's section on prorogation.)

BTR also uses discharge reports to avoid re-reviewing bills amended at third reading on the floor. Technically, a bill amended at this time should be back to BTR for review of the amendment, but this seldom happens.

When the BTR finally releases a bill, it is then ready for its third and final reading. If BTR never releases a bill, its title is still printed on the calendar every day until the session ends and the bill dies.

Third Reading of the Bill.   At the third reading, the Clerk again reads the bill's title from the podium, and the membership votes on whether to pass the bill to be engrossed. If the first branch votes against passage, the bill is dead for the whole session—unless someone moves to reconsider it. If the first branch votes in favor of passage, the bill will be sent to the other branch, where it must go over the same hurdles of another three-reading process. So, a House bill goes through three readings in the House and is sent to the Senate for three readings. A Senate bill gets three readings in the Senate and is sent to the House for three readings.

Both branches must pass the bill in exactly the same form before it can be enacted into law. If the second branch amends the bill in any way, the bill returns to the first branch which must give its concurrence to the amended version. Lacking concurrence, a conference committee is appointed to work out a bill which both branches will adopt. This committee is comprised of six members—three senators appointed by the President and three representatives appointed by the Speaker.

Bills which are amended at the third reading in the second branch must return to the first branch and repeat the whole three-reading process there again. Nine readings and votes (six in the first branch and three in the second)—a lobbyist's nightmare!

After each branch passes the bill to be engrossed, the bill goes to the Engrossing Division for **engrossment.** (Logical, isn't it?) Engrossment is the printing of a bill on special paper in the exact form in which it passed in both branches. The Engrossing Division is an office established by statute under the direct supervision of the House and Senate Clerks.

Enactment.   After it's actually engrossed, the bill is sent to the House and then the Senate for enactment. Usually this is a formality, but occasionally a controversial bill will be debated (and even rejected) at the enactment stage. An engrossed bill in enactment stage cannot be amended, unless it has been returned by the Governor with recommendations for amendments. In that case, one branch will engross it as amended by the Governor and then send it to the other branch for concurrence.

Sometimes bills contain **emergency preambles** stating why they must take effect immediately rather than after the typical ninety- or thirty-day waiting period. (See Chapter 9 for more on ninety- and thirty-day bills.) Preambles require a standing vote (members literally stand up and are counted) separate from the vote on the bill. This vote occurs after engrossment but before the vote on enactment. This preamble must pass by a 2/3 majority in each house. If either branch rejects the preamble, both branches then vote on enactment of the bill itself. If it passes, it becomes effective after the usual thirty- or ninety-day period. The vote to enact the bill must pass by a simple majority.

These are the formal steps a bill takes from committee to enactment. Think of them as a game board; the bill must pass through all these boxes on the board before reaching the end square. This is the big picture. But the game is actually played in small steps. The next section describes how the players move around the board.

The Day-to-Day Routine

Formal sessions of the Massachusetts House and Senate are usually held only three days a week: Mondays, Tuesdays, and Wednesdays. Each branch holds informal sessions on Thursdays to act on noncontroversial bills on which the leadership expects no debate. Usually no sessions are held on Fridays. During budget debate and prior to prorogation, however, there are sometimes formal sessions every day of the week, including Saturdays and Sundays. Forty-eight hour marathons during budget debates and prorogation are not uncommon.

Formal sessions in the House and Senate are divided into three parts:

1. motions from the floor that are made or taken up before proceeding with the Orders of the Day,
2. the Orders of the Day, and
3. floor action on the Orders of the Day.

The President and the Speaker customarily begin each session with a prayer by the official Chaplin or a guest preacher, followed by informal consultations with their leadership team, members of the minority leadership, or any legislator hanging around the rostrum seeking a "word or two." After granting those audiences, the gavel is banged again and the question comes, "Is there any objection to proceeding with the Orders of the Day?"

At this time members wishing to reconsider a vote made in the previous session will rise and offer that motion. This is also the proper time to offer motions to amend the rules and to hear reports from the Committee on Rules issuing resolutions and committee extensions. While these motions are customarily approved by voice vote, whenever the minority party or an individual disgruntled legislator offers and forces debate on controversial orders, the debate can go on for hours.

The President and the Speaker proceed with the Orders of the

Day by beginning on page 1 of the Daily Calendar. Beside each stands the Clerk of their branch in charge of special metal boxes holding the bills and petitions stacked in order of the calendar. (A rare opportunity for the public to see real bills.) The Clerk follows the Speaker and the President with the calendar, pulling each bill and reading out loud the bill's title and lead sponsor. While sometimes whole pages are skipped because the bills listed are still held in BTR, those bills that are released from BTR are announced by the Speaker or President and read (only the title) by the Clerk. If members wish to debate or amend the bill, or even delay action for an hour or two, they signify their wish to do so by calling out "pass" after the Clerk finishes. If no member calls out, the President or the Speaker will call for a voice vote by droning, "All in favor say aye, all opposed say no. The ayes have it; the bill is ordered to be engrossed." This little speech is accompanied by a simultaneous banging of the gavel and takes two seconds. Sometimes a happy sponsor will shout out an aye, but voice votes do not require real voices.

The next category of bills are those appearing on the calendar for their second reading. The Clerk reads the bill title and, if no legislators calls out "pass," the two-second speech ends with "the bill is ordered to a third reading."

The final group of bills on the calendar are adverse reports from committees. The question posed by the Speaker or the President is, "Should the report of the committee be accepted?" Unless someone calls out, "pass," the report is accepted on a voice vote.

Bills and adverse reports "passed over" are then debated in order of their appearance on the calendar.

Once a week, the Senate calendar lists those bills that have been tabled during previous sessions. Both the House and the Senate also list bills scheduled for debate on a date certain in the future.

During the reading of the Orders of the Day, the galleries are full of lobbyists and staff marking off their own calendars and intently watching the activities around the rostrum. For the most part the "regulars" in both the House and Senate are very generous about sharing information with novice lobbyists who cannot translate the gibberish that comes from the rostrum or understand the significance of the animated discussion going on around it. You will flatter any regular's expertise by asking him or her to explain what happened, but be careful to wait for a break in the action to ask, or you could get your head bitten off.

Once the calendar has been finished, all items passed over are taken up in order. Often there is extended debate, amendments are offered, roll calls are held, and various parliamentary maneu-

---

20

staggering borrowing costs imposed on the taxpayers of the Commonwealth as a result of the $1.225 billion dollars borrowed to underwrite the current state budget debt by immediately ceasing their use of the state pension fund as an executive free cash account.
[Laid over under the provisions of Senate Rule 27C.]
[15 minutes debate — 3 minutes per Senator.]
► [*Vote required:*— Two-thirds of the members present and voting.] ◄

The Following Matters Are Appearing On the Senate Calendar For the First Time.

756. [S. 290] Bill prohibiting the use of commercial nuclear power plants not in operation before August 1, 1987 for providing electric power within the Commonwealth (Senate, No. 290). **2d.** [Costello.]
[Representative Bradford of Rochester dissents.]
[From the committee on Energy.]
[From the committee on Steering and Policy-*Keating.*]

757. [S. 1015] Bill requiring the installation of sprinkler systems in certain buildings occupied by elderly persons (Senate, No. 1015). **2d.** [Albano.]
[From the committee on Public Safety.]
[*The committee on Ways and Means (Walsh) recommends* that the bill be amended by striking out section 2 and inserting in place thereof the following new section: —
"SECTION 2. The provisions of section one shall not apply to a building constructed under a building permit issued prior to January first, nineteen hundred and eighty-nine.".]
[From the committee on Steering and Policy-*Keating.*]

758. [S. 1051] Bill further regulating the sale of firearms, rifles, shotguns and ammunition (Senate, No. 1051). **2d.** [Albano.]
[From the committee on Public Safety.]
[From the committee on Steering and Policy-*Keating.*]

759. [S. 1191] Bill authorizing the deputy commissioner of the Division of Capital Planning and Operations to lease space on behalf of the University of Massachusetts at Worcester (Senate, No. 1191). **2d.** [Reilly-Bertonazzi.]
[From the committees on State Administration and Ways and Means.]
[From the committee on Steering and Policy-*Keating.*]

A page from a calendar showing a lobbyist's notes in the margin.

vers are attempted to advance or stop bills. Some items passed over earlier move forward on voice votes because the member concerned had a chance to read the bill or have his questions answered by the sponsor. It looks like a legislature right out of the civics books.

21

760. [S. 1218] Bill authorizing the Board of Commissioners of the Dalton Fire District to convey certain land in the town of Windsor to the Commonwealth of Massachusetts through its Division of Fisheries and Wildlife (Senate, No. 1218). **2d.** [Reilly.]
[From the committee on State Administration.]
[*The committee on Ways and Means (Webber) recommends* that the bill be amended in section 1 by inserting after the word "its", in line 3, the words "division of capital planning and operations in consultation with".]
[From the committee on Steering and Policy-*Keating.*]

761. [S. 1519] Bill relative to retirement benefits for Philip Turchin (Senate, No. 1519). **2d.** [Golden.]
[Substituted by amendment by the Senate (Harold) for the report of the committee on Public Service, ought NOT to pass, on petition.]
[From the committee on Counties on the part of the Senate.]
[From the committee on Steering and Policy-*Keating.*]

762. [S. 1546] Bill increasing the number of assistant clerks in East Boston District Court (Senate, No. 1546). **2d.** [LoPresti-Walsh.]
[From the committees on the Judiciary and Ways and Means.]
[From the committee on Steering and Policy-*Keating.*]

763. [S. 1618] Bill further defining the license required for the purchase of firearms and ammunition (Senate, No. 1618). **2d.** [Albano.]
[On Senate, No. 1050.]
[From the committee on Public Safety.]
[From the committee on Steering and Policy-*Keating.*]

764. [S. 1634] Bill clarifying the duty of licensed mental health professionals to take precautions against patient violence (Senate, No. 1634). **2d.** [Houston-Bertonazzi.]
[On Senate, No. 521.]
[From the committees on Human Services and Elderly Affairs and Ways and Means.]
[From the committee on Steering and Policy-*Keating.*]

Continued.

When the calendar is finished, the Speaker (or the President) accepts a motion "ordering the House (or Senate) to meet next on the following . . .," and then accepts an order to adjourn. Sometimes there is a considerable wait between those two motions, and members and observers in the gallery leave, thinking the day's business is over. Experienced lobbyists watching a controversial item on the calendar stay until the motion to adjourn is accepted. Many a rule has been suspended and many a bill has been amended between the motion ordering the next session and the motion to adjourn.

Both the House and the Senate print an official journal of their proceedings. "Unproofed" copies of the previous day's journal, as well as past issues, are available for your reading pleasure only in the offices of the House and Senate Clerks. (The staff will make limited copies of vital pages.) Final copies are eventually available in the Document Room.

Deliberations

Now you know the game board and the general method of playing the game. But on each turn, players can make many different kinds of moves. This section describes all the possible floor maneuvers.

Debate

Debate may occur on the questions of ordering a bill to third reading, passing it to be engrossed or to be enacted. Debate occurs most often on the question of ordering a bill to third reading. Many bills are ordered to third reading, and most engrossed bills are passed to be enacted, without debate.

In addition, many procedural tactics described below are subject to debate. Usually debate on the merits of a bill has no time limit. But on many parliamentary points of order, debate is often limited or completely prohibited. In the House, debate can be stopped if a motion to end debate carries with a simple majority; then debate ends thirty minutes after the motion passes. The Senate has a similar rule which allows one hour of debate after a motion to end debate is adopted.

Voting

There are several different voting methods in each branch.

Voice Votes. The most common type, a voice vote theoretically means that the members say yes or no, and the Speaker or the President declares the winner based on what he hears. In fact, most voice votes are silent; no one says anything and the Speaker announces the result he wants.

Sometimes voice votes are inconclusive. The Speaker or President may be unable to decide the issue, or a member may object to the result by saying, "I doubt the vote." When either of these events occur, other kinds of voting will follow the voice vote.

A Standing Vote. After a voice vote, the chair can ask for a **standing vote** (also called a **division of the house**). Then the members stand to be counted for or against the bill.

Roll Call Vote. Any member may request a **roll call** vote. In the House, twenty members must stand in favor of the request; in the Senate, eight supporters are needed. This request most often comes from a member who supports a bill or motion which just lost on a voice or standing vote. Less frequently, the request comes from a member who thinks the issue is important enough to get his or her colleagues on the record on a controversial item.

In the House, roll call votes are counted electronically; each member pushes a lever at his chamber desk and a green light indicating "yes" or a red light indicating "no" appears next to his or her name on a large scoreboard at the front of the chamber.

Members must actually be present to vote. An ill or disabled House member may vote from his/her office by calling the Speaker. The Speaker announces the member's presence in the building and instructs a court officer to push the appropriate lever at the member's desk.

In the Senate, roll call votes are called out. The clerk reads the senators' names alphabetically, and each member says yes or no. Those who miss their names can ask for recognition later. Usually, Senate roll calls take fifteen minutes, but some tallies have been kept open for hours waiting for the vote of an absent senator. With unanimous consent of the senators present on the floor, an absent member's vote can be recorded by "**pairing**" it with the vote of an attending member. In this case, the present member voting for the bill pairs him or herself with the absent member who has voted against it—or vice versa. The two votes cancel each other out and are not counted in the final tally. But the constituents of both senators can see how they voted. The request for the pair comes from the attending member. Pairing rarely takes place during hotly contested votes. Senators can also change their votes before the role call closes.

Amendments

Bills can be amended at second or third reading but not at the enactment stage. Amendments must be "within the scope" of the original bill, which means they must concern the areas of the law already defined in the bill. Applying this definition to a particular bill is sometimes difficult; often the boundaries are unclear and there are many areas of gray. These decisions are made by the Speaker or the Senate President. There is no limit on the number of amendments which may be proposed to a single bill. In fact, members can (and do) propose amendments to amendments.

Reconsideration

Almost any action taken on the floor of the House or Senate may be reconsidered. There are two parts to reconsideration. First, any member may move (request) reconsideration of an action. Second, a majority of the members present must vote for reconsideration. Then the original action will be voted on again. Members must request reconsideration no later than the next day after the action was taken and before the calendar is read the next day.

The vote on a reconsideration request sometimes occurs immediately and sometimes at the next formal working session. It is delayed when the request pertains to a vote on passage of a whole bill. But if the request pertains to a subsidiary question, such as an amendment or a point of parliamentary procedure, then the vote to reconsider happens immediately: (1) when a member requests suspension of the rules in order to reconsider it on the same day that the action in question occurred; and (2) during prorogation. (See this chaper's section on prorogation for more rules changes at this time.)

Postponement

In either branch, a majority vote can postpone action on a bill. Action can be postponed to: (1) the end of the calendar; (2) to a specific time; or (3) to a specific date.

Tabling

In the Senate, if a majority of the members vote to **lay the matter on the table**, action on a bill is postponed indefinitely. Once laid on the table, a bill cannot be considered until a majority of the members vote to take it off the table. By custom (although the rules do not specify this), only the senator who moved to table the bill can later ask to remove it (as in the example at the beginning of this chapter). Opponents often use tabling motions in the Senate to kill bills (see this chapter's section on "The Vote").

A motion to table a bill is automatically postponed to the next working session—unless the rules are suspended so it can be taken up immediately (as in the opening section of this chapter). During prorogation, tabling motions are always voted on right away.

Committing or Recommitting a Bill to Committee

In either branch, a majority vote can send a bill to a committee which has not previously reviewed it, or can recommit a bill to its original committee. When a bill is sent back to a joint committee, the committee must act on it within the time limits required by the rules for bills originally referred to that committee. (Joint committees must make a final report by the fourth Wednesday in April for all bills referred to them before April 15, and within ten days on all matters referred to them after April 15. See Chapter 4 section on deadlines.)

Suspension of the Rules

Any rule, except those imposed by the Constitution or statute, can be suspended. Most require a 2/3 vote of members present, although some require a 4/5 vote or a unanimous agreement.

Second Legislative Day

Occasionally, in order to get around the requirement that certain actions be automatically postponed to the next day (such as reconsideration or laying a bill on the table), the House or Senate will vote to adjourn and meet again the same day. This is known as a **second legislative day.** It is often done during fiscal crises or when the leadership knows it has the votes one day, but thinks it won't have them the next. It requires only a majority vote.

Points of Order

When a member believes a rule has been violated, he or she can ask the chair to enforce the rule. The member must stand, say "point of order," and describe the rule being violated. The Speaker or President then decides if there has been a violation. A member who disagrees with the decision can request a vote on the ruling, but the request must be supported (seconded) by at least one other member.

Point of Personal Privilege

Occasionally a member will stand and state, "point of personal privilege," indicating that he or she wants the Speaker or President to decide whether his or her rights or reputation have been called into question. The point is rarely granted because no one knows what it really means or what action should follow. Nonetheless, it's frequently used to delay debate or to embarrass the chair.

Referral to Supreme Judicial Court (SJC)

The constitution allows the legislature to send important questions, such as the constitutionality of a major bill, to the SJC for an advisory opinion. Often the legislature uses this rule to postpone action on a bill until the SJC delivers its opinion. The SJC may refuse to answer.

The Vote

THE MORE CONFUSED AND BAFFLED YOU ARE, THE CLOSER YOU ARE TO ENLIGHTENMENT. (Buddha)

Now that you know some of the tactics that are at the disposal of members of the House and Senate, the next step is learning how to use them to your best advantage. Let's set the stage by reminding you that you already know more than most people about the legislative process, the leadership structure, and how individual legislators vote.

Legislators come into work in the morning and are handed the calendar, which lists some 100 or so bills by title. If they are lucky enough to have good staff, the calendar is marked to indicate bills of interest, and there is a file folder with fact sheets and memos regarding the marked items. Legislators who wish to debate any item on the calendar go down to the session at 1:00 p.m. Others proceed with their schedule: committee hearings to testify or sit and listen; meetings with constituents or lobbyists; membership caucus meetings; a long-awaited meeting with the leadership; briefing sessions with policy staff; lunch with local dignitaries; the visiting fifth grade class from the local elementary school.

Sooner or later the word comes: roll call in six minutes. On the way to the chamber, the legislator may look at the calendar and ask, "What's this about—and what's my vote?" If the calendar item is marked, the legislator reads the reminder, votes, and leaves. Those who have no idea what the bill is about must rely on information from the leadership, the legislator sitting in the next seat, or the sponsor or the opposition (who may or may not be moving around the chamber pleading their case). Unlobbied legislators must figure out the safest vote before they can leave.

Lobbyist briefing a floor leader before debate.

Scary, isn't it? Well, pilgrims, that's they way it happens absent a lobbying campaign. As anecdotal evidence, here are two versions of the same vote. In the first version, there are no citizen lobbyists. The second version shows how things can change when a lobbying campaign is in place.

Version I

It is 3:30 on Wednesday afternoon, and the House is in formal session. Only thirty-seven members are in the chamber; two of them are debating a bill that would ban whale hunting off the Massachusetts coast. The Speaker is absorbed in an animated conversation with a visiting dignitary from Washington. The Minority Leader is on the phone. The rest of the members are reading their mail or chatting with their colleagues. Nobody appears to be listening to the so-called debate between the sponsor (a hardworking young representative with a specialty in environmental issues) and the chair of the committee considering the bill (a staunch believer in the free enterprise system who sees this bill as a serious threat to it).

The debate ends, the Speaker asks for a vote, and the nays have it. When the sponsor doubts the vote, roll call is announced. "Roll call in the House in five minutes" comes over the loudspeakers in the lunchroom, some committee hearing rooms, and in individual offices. Routine phone calls are made to other private offices, meeting rooms in the State House, and to the Golden Dome bar across the street.

Representatives immediately stop what they are doing, leave staff meetings, constituent meetings, committee hearings, and lunch to fill up the House chamber. As they enter, they check the electronic roll call board for the number of the bill being debated and check their calendars to find out the bill's title. If they don't know what the bill is about, they ask others who do. By looking at the votes already cast on the board, they figure out who the sponsor is and who supports and opposes the bill. If most of the people voting for the bill are colleagues they respect and like, and if the bill is something that sounds reasonable, they vote with their colleagues and leave the chamber.

But if the leadership asks them *not* to, they usually weigh what they know about the bill against the risks of opposing the Speaker. Usually the Speaker wins—in part, because he bothered to ask; and, in part, because each time a representative goes along with the leadership, he or she has improved his or her chances for a return favor later in the session. A pet local bill may get unstuck, the representative's staff person may get a pay raise, or the chance for a vice-chairmanship comes sooner rather than later. Since the leadership opposes this bill, it will probably fail to pass.

Version II

Fifty-five members of the House are present in the chamber. Five of them have already spoken in support of a bill to ban whale hunting. The floor leader of the opposition glances up repeatedly at the galleries, where ten people sit wearing day-glo stickers printed with "Vote yes on H.1234—Save the Whales." There are more of them outside the chamber, handing out fact sheets, and most of the members on the floor are telling him they've been committed on this particular bill since they met with a small group of environmentalists from the district last fall. Nevertheless the floor leader takes the podium to debate against the bill, and asks for a roll call.

As members come into the chamber, it is clear that they have

A floor leader on his way to debate.

already been lobbied by the proponents of the bill. "Already committed, sorry pal." "I got five phone calls yesterday telling me this bill was on the calendar, and I got a file folder with ten letters." "Listen, I've never even seen a whale, but I've seen enough whale-lovers to last a lifetime. And I gotta be with them."

Outside the chamber, most representatives tell the citizen lobbyists, "Hey, I'm with you, I'm with you." Others mutter under their breath, and a couple seek out the bill's lobbyist to ask a technical question or to complain about the number of nutty calls they've been getting. They ask the lobbyist to call off the constituents; they've been committed on this bill since November and are sick of people who seem to doubt their word. The lobbyist says that as soon as the roll call is over, the local people will be contacted to write a press release to the local paper saying what swell fellows they are. The representatives quiet down and think about whether to go into the chamber and help in the debate. Maybe they'll even try to call off the leadership.

The Speaker—observing the presence of the Committee to Protect Whales in the gallery and listening to seven committee chairmen say they're "getting heat from the district on this one"—decides he doesn't *really* care about killing this bill after all. He then releases everyone else. The final is 120-22 and the gallery erupts into applause.

How Did the Committee to Protect Whales Do It?

Remember the two rules of lobbying:

1. Lobbying is getting the right information to the right people at the right time.
2. Elected decision makers make different decisions when watched by the affected constituency.

A good lobbyist is often able to get a week or a few day's notice before the bill appears on the calendar. This is all the time you'll have to plan and pull off your floor strategy. You can get the maximum advance notice by keeping in close contact with the bill's sponsors and the staff of the joint committee which originally reported out your bill. Sponsors can ask the committee chairman for advance notice and can alert the Clerk's office of their interest. The staff does the paperwork on the bill and knows when it was delivered to the Clerk's office.

When you know the date for floor action, then you must pull together the two lists that have been building all along and notify everyone on each list (a very busy few days).

The first list includes all the members of the branch to which the bill will be reported. Next to each name should be notes indicating which members are (1) sponsors, (2) solid supporters, (3) leaning yes's, (4) undecideds, (5) leaning no's, (6) solid opponents, and (7) don't knows. First, notify all sponsors and solid supporters to rebrief them and their staffs on the bill, to give them the latest information, and to send them another copy of the bill (they will have lost it). The leaning yes's, undecideds, and don't knows should get a copy of the fact sheet, lists of sponsors and allies (inside and outside), and a note that the bill will be on the calendar soon. Obviously, leaning no's and solid opposition should get no advance warning.

Next, the lobbyist works with the sponsors to figure out if the bill will be debated. If debate is expected, one of the sponsors must agree to be a **floor leader.** The floor leader takes primary responsibility for "carrying" the bill. He or she speaks first, summarizing the issues and coordinating the response to the opponents. Finally, the floor leader and the lobbyist organize a **floor team** from the list of supporters. The team should have four or five sparkling debaters with loads of personal credibility or special expertise.

The second list includes names of the legislative network of the affected constituency. However you contact them—by mail or by phone—the message is the same. "Our bill, H.1234, will be on the House calendar on Tuesday or Wednesday. Please *call* your rep (or senator) *today* and remind him or her that you hope he or she will remember to vote with you." If this all works, the members will get phone calls from constituents at the same time the lobbyist is sending them fact sheets. This is a good time to send a delegation from the organization to the State House to help distribute materials and to be visible in general.

The Question: To Debate or Not to Debate?

If your bill is not controversial, and you do not expect debate, don't go looking for it. Sometimes groups want a debate and roll call vote so that the legislators' vote will be on record with their constituents. But a member who doesn't object to the results of a voice vote can also be recorded as favoring the bill. Remember the poker player's song:

> *"Know when to hold 'em*
> *Know when to fold 'em*
> *Know when to walk away,*
> *Know when to run."*

In this case, take your voice vote and run!

If your bill is controversial and opponents are organized to fight it, you have no choice: You must prepare to debate. The lobbyist should brief the floor team on the opponents' arguments and your

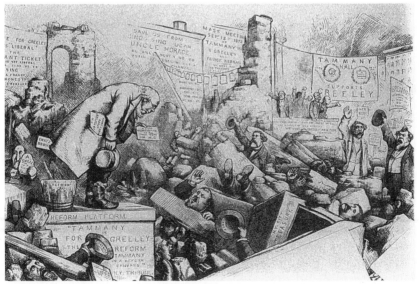

D-Day. A floor leader must be prepared to snap back with counter-strategies.

side's best counterarguments. The floor leader should be armed with acceptable compromises in amendment form before debate begins.

At this time, you must also consider whether more time is needed to marshal support on the floor or whether more media attention would help. If so, discuss with the floor leader which delaying tactics would work best. Should you get the debate postponed for a day, a week, or two weeks? Or recommitted to a friendly committee that will report it back out in ten days?

If, instead of delay, you want to get it out fast, the floor team must be prepared to fight any delaying tactics by the opposition. Also you must work especially hard to get whoever is in the chair to wield a fast and supportive gavel. Perhaps the chair could even be persuaded to suspend a rule or two.

Preparing for a Roll Call

If you expect a debate, you should also expect a roll call vote. To prepare for this, the lobbyist should divide up the names of all leaning yes's, undecideds, and don't knows between the floor team and a delegation from the organization. Someone should talk individually with each person on this list. Then move on to the list of leaning no's. Solid supporters should get only a short note reminding them of the vote and thanking them for their help to date. Don't spend valuable time phoning them. And forget the solid no's altogether.

Don't be discouraged by the size of this job and the short amount of time you have to do it. Even if you can't reach everyone, talk to as many members as possible.

"D-Day"

On the day of the debate and expected roll call, the lobbyist and a delegation from the organization hang around in the area outside the House or Senate chamber, reminding supporters of their commitments and making last-minute pitches to undecided members. By this time, the lobbyist and the organization members should have condensed their problem and the bill's proposed solution into a fifteen-second pitch, such as, "Save whales off the Massachusetts coast by voting 'yes' for H.1234." Again, avoid wasting time by arguing with opponents.

The activity described above is what most people think of as lobbying—probably because it takes place in the lobby. But if your organization waits until this moment to influence the legislative process, you will be wasting your time. All the preparation described in the preceding chapters must be done for this moment to have any impact.

Once the debate on your bill begins, the lobbyist must be instantly available for consultation with the floor leader and floor team. Legislators are used to signaling up to lobbyists sitting in the gallery for a quick conference outside the chamber. As your opponents cast stumbling blocks your way—amendments, attempts at postponement, or reconsideration—you and your team must snap back with counterstrategies. You may have to change plans suddenly. During this stage, it's good to have a technical expert on hand to rebut proposed amendments from the opposition.

Floor action often moves quickly. With only one pair of eyes, it's hard to keep track of everything that's happening. Members from the organization can help by (1) watching action on floor, (2) conferring with the floor team, and (3) carrying messages between the floor team and the lobbyist.

Conclusion

Although we've used a lot of space to describe procedural rules, intimate knowledge of these rules is *not* the key to influencing floor action. Anybody can buy a rule book, or confer with the Clerk's office. The key to influencing floor action starts with the identification of the affected constituency and the choice of credible and competent sponsors. It ends with the mobilization of that constituency into an effective legislative network and with briefing and rebriefing the floor leader and team.

Prorogation

During prorogation—a process (sometimes three weeks long or more) that ends with the formal closing of the legislative session for the year—many procedural rules are changed or abandoned. Under the Massachusetts Constitution, in order to end the session leadership in each branch and the Governor must all agree that the legislature has concluded its business for the year. This gives each of the three parties a great deal of leverage on the other two. If the Governor wants a certain piece of legislation to be passed in the current session, he can simply refuse to allow prorogation. Similarly, the Senate President or the Speaker can refuse to prorogue until certain bills are passed in the opposite branch.

Lobbying during prorogation is more difficult for several reasons. A mood of urgency descends upon the legislature. Both branches change their procedures to push bills through—*fast!* They suspend all "slowing-down" rules, thus speeding up the whole process. Calendars are not required: Reconsideration and tabling motions are taken up immediately, and limits on debate are shortened.

Second, more and more of the action takes place behind the scenes as the legislative leaders and the Governor decide which bills will pass and which will die before the session ends. Traditionally, the Speaker, the Senate President, and the Governor each prepares his own "must list" of legislation and then bargains formally and informally with the other two. ("I'll agree to get your stuff out, if you'll give me mine.") Legislators and lobbyists do their best to get their own pet bills onto at least one must-list—although it's difficult. At prorogation, the leadership is preoccupied with their own legislative priorities and the political strategies necessary to win them. Even the minority leaders will have short must-lists and will succeed in getting a bill or two passed in exchange for sacrificing some debate on the majority's legislation.

Third, sessions are long and punctuated by recesses. They are long because one of leadership's tactics to cool out their opposition is to simply wear them down by twelve-hour sessions day after day, usually climaxing in a thirty-six-hour marathon. They are filled with recesses because the leadership meets frequently to negotiate and renegotiate the must-list with determined and aggressive opponents—and sometimes even with special interest groups.

The absence of a regular calendar forces lobbyists (and their network people) to monitor all floor sessions in order to find out which bills are being released from committee. Someone must be there to hear the Clerk or the chair read the bill titles. Legislation comes tumbling out of Bills on Third Reading and Ways and Means at all times of day and night. Must-list bills will actually pass both branches and arrive on the Governor's desk before the legislature prorogues; bills not on these lists will somehow "fall short" of final enactment or will never get to the top of the pile in the Engrossing Division. These occurrences are *not* accidents. Most legislators and lobbyists know that a good way to get credit with the folks back home is to claim that a favorite bill "almost made it" during prorogation and then blame the failure on the Clerk's office or the leadership. Don't let them fool *you.*

If your bill begins to move during prorogation, you may begin to hope for a last-minute victory. And it may happen, though the odds are against it. In general, don't count on the craziness of proro-gation to get your bill through unless you can get it onto a must-list. Whenever possible, get it passed earlier in the session.

Thank Yous

After the vote, the lobbyists and the network should send thank you notes to the floor leader, the floor team members, and any other outstanding heroes in your campaign. Did the Speaker gavel through an important suspension of the rules? Did an opponent *finally* yield graciously? Did the Clerk answer thirteen different questions from the lobbyist? Send them all notes. They will remem-ber it in next year's efforts.

An especially effective tactic is to organize your legislative net-work to write thank you notes to their own legislators.

Chapter 6

THE GOVERNOR

After a bill has been passed to be enacted in both branches, it is sent to the Governor.

What the Governor Can Do

In Massachusetts, the Governor has several options for action on each bill.

Sign.   He (or, someday, she) has ten days to sign the bill; then it becomes law.

Veto.   He can reject the bill and return it to the branch where it originated. In this case, the Governor must state in writing his objections to the bill.

Amend.   He can return the bill to the branch where it originated, with recommendations that amendments be made.

Allow It to Become Law Without His Signature.   He can also do nothing; after ten days (if the legislature is still in session), the bill becomes law without the Governor's signature.

Pocket Veto.   If the Governor takes no action upon receiving a bill and the legislature adjourns before ten days are up, the bill does not become law.

Emergency Preamble.   If the Governor signs a bill into law, he may also attach an **emergency preamble** to it, making it effective immediately. Although the legislature must have a 2/3 majority vote in each branch to pass an emergency preamble (see Chapter 5 for more on emergency preambles), the Governor can do this independently without approval by any other body.

How the Legislature Responds

If the Governor Vetoes: Voting to Override

If the Governor vetoes a bill, it returns to the branch where it originated. There, if 2/3 of the members vote to override the veto, the bill is sent to the other branch. If 2/3 of the members in the second branch also vote to override, the bill becomes law—despite the Governor's veto.

The legislature can vote to override a veto at any time before the session prorogues, or they may never do so at all. If either branch fails to override the veto, the measure is dead for the year. If the override vote fails in the first branch, it will not even be sent to the second branch.

If the Governor Amends

When the Governor returns the bill with proposed amendments, the legislature can: (1) adopt the amendments (or any other amendments offered) and reenact the bill; or (2) reenact the bill in its original form. The renacted bill is then sent back to the Governor. The Governor cannot recommend amendments a second time, but must sign, veto, or allow the bill to become law without signature.

As with the veto, there is no deadline for the legislature to adopt or reject the Governor's amendments. Amended bills can be left hanging indefinitely. These bills die when the legislature prorogues.

Getting More Time: Requesting a Recall

In this procedure, a senator requests that a bill already enacted by both branches be recalled from the Governor's desk and returned to the Senate. Bills are recalled when: (1) the Governor or the leadership wants one more shot at amending them; or (2) either of these parties wants more than the allotted ten days to bargain over the Governor's signature.

Usually recalled bills are sent right back to the Governor for another ten days. Occasionally they are amended in the Senate. An amended bill must be reenacted in both the House and the Senate before landing back on the Governor's desk.

Lobbying the Governor

The Governor makes the final decision on your bill, so lobbyists must do whatever they can to get his signature, even if the Governor has opposed your issues in the past. Conversely, don't count on automatic support from a Governor who appears to be an ally or has supported your previously filed bills. Find out what his stance is on this one.

Who Influences the Governor?

The Staff.   Like legislators, the Governor has staff people. Every Governor has a legislative office, including legislative counsel, which recommends final action on bills. The agencies and departments concerned with the subject matter of the bill also influence the Governor's decision. Many of these agencies have their own **legislative liaisons,** whose function is to watch bills moving through the process. (Yes, this is a fancy name for—you guessed it—*lobbyists!*)

Identify sympathetic staff members in all these offices. These staff members can help you by (1) providing backup information to support your case; (2) recommending that the executive branch lobby for your bill in the legislature; (3) telling you whether or not the executive branch will oppose it and how active that opposition may be; and (4) urging the Governor to sign it when it finally reaches his desk.

The governor has a legislative office which recommends final action on bills.

Lobbying the Governor's staff is similar to lobbying legislative staff. Find out who has the most influence and information and keep in touch with them. Give them accurate, up-to-date information on your issue.

But be realistic about what staff people can and cannot do for you. They are highly mobile, changing jobs often (especially at lower staff levels), and going quickly in and out of favor with their bosses. *Their first loyalties are always to their bosses.* Regardless of their personal views on your issue, they may not be able to help you if that help would conflict with the Governor's goals. Also some staff aides can influence their boss' outlooks on one issue, but not on others.

Remember that your issue is only one of the jillion they must deal with. They may be able to help you a little bit, but don't expect them to lobby everyone they know for you. That's your job.

Legislators.   Governors also respond to pressure from certain legislators, personal friends, and political supporters as well as from the legislative leadership. It is perfectly appropriate to ask one of these legislators to speak to the Governor on behalf of your bill. It doesn't hurt to get as many legislators as possible to communicate with the Governor—especially if you fear a veto. In this case, try to make the Governor believe you could get enough votes to override it. Politicians always think twice about picking a fight they might lose.

Other Influences.   Most Governors have a "kitchen cabinet"— old friends and family members who give them solicited and unsolicited advice on how to manage the state. If you can get one of these people to champion your cause, now is the time for him/her to go to bat for you. This is also a good time to mobilize a letter-writing campaign from allies and supporters to demonstrate broad-based support for your bill.

Finally, Governors are very sensitive to the pressures of the media. If your bill is a public issue, bring on the editorials urging him to sign. If your bill is a nonpublic issue, try to get the State House press to at least *ask* the Governor's staff whether or not he will sign it. If the staff thinks he'll get some good press by signing your bill, they'll pay more attention to it and may urge him to sign when the time comes.

Pressures on the Governor: Timing and Intensity

Your legislative network should begin communicating with the Governor to urge him to sign the bill as soon as it passes in both branches. Whether or not you organize a huge effort before the bill

THE COMMONWEALTH OF MASSACHUSETTS
EXECUTIVE DEPARTMENT
STATE HOUSE   •   BOSTON 02133

MICHAEL S. DUKAKIS
GOVERNOR

To ensure a balanced budget in Fiscal Year 1988, the Governor is vetoing or reducing "prior appropriations continued" in the following items in the FY89 General Appropriations Act:

ACCOUNT	ACCOUNT DESCRIPTION	ACTION	REDUCE PAC TO	ESTIMATED SAVINGS
0111-8000	SENATE MEMBERS	Reduce PAC	24,014	50,000
0112-0000	SENATE CLERK	Reduce PAC	45,765	80,000
0112-0100	SENATE PRINTING	Veto PAC	*	18,550
0114-0000	SENATE COUNSEL	Veto PAC	*	164,654
0115-0000	SENATE AIDES	Veto PAC	*	1,279,857
0116-0000	SENATE SECRETARIAL & CLERICAL	Veto PAC	*	624,646
0116-0030	SENATE INTERN PROGRAM	Veto PAC	*	37,250
0118-0000	SENATE SUPPLIES	Veto PAC	*	621,442
0119-0000	SENATE ART COMM REPAIR	Veto PAC	*	173,565
0131-0000	SERGEANT AT ARMS ADMIN	Veto PAC	*	149,700
0132-1000	CLERKS, DOCUMENT ROOM	Veto PAC	*	6,000
0133-0000	LEGIS CONTINGENT EXPENSE	Veto PAC	*	171
0135-0000	ROLL CALL EXPENSES	Veto PAC	*	13,750
0142-0000	LEGIS RESEARCH BUREAU	Veto PAC	*	105,890
0145-0000	SENATE COMM SERVICES	Veto PAC	*	781,992
0147-0000	LEGIS ENGROSSING DIV	Reduce PAC	55,393	26,032
0161-2000	STATE HOUSE PHYSICIAN	Reduce PAC	4,000	2,405
0163-0000	JOINT COMM, ADMIN	Reduce PAC	30,000	55,671
0165-0000	NAT'L CONF OF LEGIS LEADERS	Veto PAC	*	21,200
0169-7102	SENATE POST AUDIT	Veto PAC	*	143,609
0185-7209	JOINT COMM UNIFORM SENTENCING	Veto PAC	*	13,950
0185-7509	MEDICAL MALPRACTICE STUDY	Veto PAC	*	75,950
0185-7801	HAZARDOUS WASTE STUDY	Veto PAC	*	77,540
0185-7803	LOCAL AID DISTRIBUTION STUDY	Veto PAC	*	28,815
0185-7804	BOSTON HARBOR SPECIAL COMN	Veto PAC	*	14,755
0185-7810	WATER SUPPLY STUDY	Veto PAC	*	7,100
0185-7814	RETIREMENT LAW SPECIAL COMM	Veto PAC	*	109,700
0185-7815	PUBLIC SCHOOL SYSTEM STUDY	Veto PAC	*	70,190
0185-7819	ALCOHOL & DRUG ABUSE SP COMN	Veto PAC	*	42,780
0185-7820	INDOOR AIR POLLUTION	Veto PAC	*	11,130
0185-7821	VIOLENCE VS CHILDREN STUDY	Veto PAC	*	23,730
0185-7823	COMPARABLE WORTH STUDY	Veto PAC	*	40,800

A governor's veto message.

reaches the Governor's desk depends on whether the bill is a public or nonpublic issue. On clearly controversial public issue bills, the Governor probably has (or will soon develop) strong feeling. You have to know them early in order to plan your strategy. If he opposes the bill, you may have to mobilize enough legislative support to override a veto.

THE COMMONWEALTH OF MASSACHUSETTS

EXECUTIVE DEPARTMENT

STATE HOUSE • BOSTON 02133

MICHAEL S. DUKAKIS
GOVERNOR

To ensure a balanced budget in Fiscal Year 1988, the Governor is vetoing or
reducing the following items in the final FY88 supplemental budget:

ACCOUNT	ACCOUNT DESCRIPTION	ACTION	REDUCE BY	REDUCE TO
0521-0000	ELECTIONS DIVISION	Veto	13,000	0
0610-6603	MCDFC, YOUTH SMALL BUSINESS	Veto	350,000	0
0612-1505	PRIT TRANSFER	Veto	3,073,239	0
1599-3671	TAX ABATEMENTS FOR SOUTHBRIDGE/FALL RIVER	Veto	56,851	0
1599-3700	IRWIN V. TOWN OF WARE	Veto	137,500	0
2050-0200	TECHNICAL ASSISTANCE	Veto	32,000	0
2120-0306	GLOUCESTER STUDY	Veto	250,000	0
2150-0600	LONG POND, TEWKSBURY	Reduce	250,000	250,000
2300-0150	ASSABET/BLACKSTONE	Veto	60,000	0
3743-2024	BLUE HILL AVENUE PLAN	Veto	150,000	0
4100-0011	MEDICARE SHORTFALL	Reduce	13,000,000	37,000,000
5048-0000	MENTAL HEALTH HOTLINE, ADVOCATES	Veto	100,000	0
6010-0051	WAREHAM HIGHWAY WORK	Veto	300,000	0
6010-0053	BROCKTON SIGNAL	Veto	15,000	0
7010-0007	EDUCATIONAL ACHIEVEMENT	Veto	75,000	0
7061-0015	REIMBURSE/REGIONAL SCHOOLS	Veto	900,000	0
7100-0100	HIGHER ED. INSTITUTIONS	Veto		
7100-0102	COUNTY COOPERATIVE EXTENSION	Veto	448,125	0
7100-0103	MASSASOIT/BANQUET FACILITY	Veto	250,000	0
7100-0105	NEW ATTLEBORO COMMUNITY COLLEGE CAMPUS	Veto	128,000	0
7100-0222	NEW MILFORD COMMUNITY COLLEGE CAMPUS	Veto	429,000	0
		Total	20,017,715	
Section 23	SOUTHWOOD HOSPITAL	Veto		
Section 26	STATE POLICE RACE TRACK ASSIGNMENTS	Veto		
Section 45	SCIENCE RESOURCE NETWORK PAC	Veto		
Section 60	LOWELL DISASTER PAC	Veto		
Section 62	HOME HEALTH AGENCIES	Veto		

Continued.

On the other hand, if your bill addresses a noncontroversial
issue, avoid much intense contact or starting too early. Either
course of action may arouse suspicion that the bill is more controversial than it appears.

Lobbying a Veto and Override

A "Message from His Excellency" containing recommended amendments or a veto will be sent directly to the appropriate Clerk's
office. (Bills originating in the House go back to the House Clerk,
and Senate bills return to the Senate Clerk.) The Speaker and the
Senate President can bring the message to the floor any time they
choose—or never.

Your sponsors should ask the leadership to bring out the message
for a vote right away if: (1) your bill has leadership support; (2) you
and your sponsors are confident of a 2/3 majority to override the
veto or the simple majority needed to defeat an amendment. If
possible, have the bill brought out along with other veto messages
that the leadership wants to override. With luck, the opposition or
the Governor won't even bother to demand a roll call vote and your
bill will win on a voice vote.

But don't count on luck. Remember those lists you used on
debate and roll call day to count up your supporters? Pull them out
of the file folders again and once more arrange the phone calls and
visits.

If you need time to build support for the override vote, your
sponsors can ask the leadership to delay bringing the message to
the floor. This delay is often needed on heretofore noncontroversial
bills that went through the whole process on voice votes, unnoticed
by most legislators until the Governor stamped his veto on them.
Many legislators may be unfamiliar with the issue and uncommitted; you may need some time to do the persuasion job necessary to
win 2/3 of them to your side. When in doubt, delay is a good idea
just to double-check your votes. The Governor's open opposition to
your bill is bound to erode or soften support in both branches, and
you'll have to shore it up again.

Sometimes that double-check reveals so much erosion in one
branch that you and your sponsors may decide to ditch the override
attempt, keep the Governor's message in the Clerks' office, and try
again next year. There is no point in forcing legislators to openly
choose to be with the Governor instead of with you. Instead of
wasting energy on this year's lost battle, start cranking up for next
year's potential victory.

Chapter 7

THE COMMITTEES ON WAYS AND MEANS AND THE STATE BUDGET

The Committees: Their Makeup and Power

Each branch has its own Ways and Means (W&M) Committee to act on bills which appropriate funds, require a new expenditure of state funds, or have some other effect on state finances. In order to carry out their special mission, the W&M Committees are organized differently from the joint committees and also follow some different procedures. Lobbying them is also somewhat different, and is addressed later in this chapter.

Power of the Ways and Means Chairs

The press always refers to the "Chairman of the powerful Ways and Means Committee." The chairs of these committees are powerful because of both the role that W&M plays in the legislature and their close ties with the leadership.

Because W&M decisions involve spending large sums of money, the leadership usually appoints loyal, competent, and discreet people to head these committees. The chair is responsible for analyzing and making recommendations on the state budget and on all bills that involve the expenditure of money. Furthermore, these recommendations must fit *into the context of the leadership's personal and political goals*. If, for example, the leadership does not want to expand community-based services, don't expect the W&M

committees to report out any bills aiding the expansion of them. But *do* expect all line items in the budget affecting those services to undergo intense scrutiny and possible reduction.

Chairs of W&M Committees often play the role of "bad guys" in the legislature. Typically, rank-and-file legislators tell constituents, "Gee, I think you've got a great little bill there. I'd vote for it, if you can ever get it out of Ways and Means." Or, "I filed a bill that would bring a housing court to our county—but Ways and Means wouldn't put it in the budget." Because W&M is the final resting place for thousands of bills, W&M chairs expect to be publicly blamed for holding them—even if they are doing so under orders from the leadership or with the blessing of the bill's sponsor, who only wanted to say that he or she filed it. (Hard to believe, but true nonetheless—there are legislators who sponsor bills in December, only to kill them in May.)

The chair is also used to arguing with angry colleagues and out-side special interest groups about W&M decisions. Arguments with outside groups are always made on the merits of the issue and rarely reveal whether the chair is acting on orders from the leader-ship or on his or her own initiative.

However, chairs of W&M *do* act on their own concerning issues in which the leadership has no great interest. Sometimes W&M chairs use their power to hold or release their colleagues' bills in order to gain support for their own pet projects. Using this power, chairs have forged major public policy decisions in matters ranging from initiating day care programs in the 1970s to reorganizing higher education in the 1980s.

Committee Members

One current member of W&M objects to the usual press identifica-tion of the chairman as "head of the powerful Ways and Means Committee." "It should be," he says, "the powerful *chairman* of the Ways and Means Committee, because nobody tells me nothing around here." It's the chairmen rather than the whole committees who have the real power. Although this member admits this pri-vately, he still uses the prestige of his appointment to the commit-tee when writing up his own campaign literature.

While committee members have no real input into W&M deci-sions, the Speaker and President need the W&M membership's public support for their positions; therefore, the committee chairs are sensitive to the needs of individual members. They regularly accommodate a few of the members' "pet" bills in return for loyalty—perhaps a new local highway bypass or a modest increase in the local mental health center's budget.

The powerful chair of Ways and Means.

On the other hand, publicly bucking the chair will definitely get a member in trouble with the leadership and could even lead to dismissal from the committee. Obviously, members try to avoid this kind of conflict.

Committee Staff

Each W&M Committee has a large hardworking staff that reports directly to the chair. The budget staff is headed by the Budget Director, who supervises 10 to 12 budget analysts, each assigned to one or more of the executive departments. The legislative staff is somewhat smaller, but generally works by issue area also; individual staff members analyze and "cost out" bills reported to W&M. Both budget and legislative staff people regularly communicate with the department staff and advocacy groups interested in bills or budget items under consideration by the committee, seeking both information and opinion from these outside parties.

Now that you understand the composition of the W&M committees, let's look at the kind of legislation they work on and how you, the lobbyist, can work with them.

The Executive Branch: Where It All Begins

Fiscal Years

Appropriations are made for fiscal, rather than for calendar, years. The Massachusetts fiscal year runs from July 1st to June 30th and is named for the year in which it ends. This means that the fiscal 1982 (often abbreviated "FY 82") budget refers to the budget for the twelve months beginning July 1st, 1981 and ending June 30th, 1982.

Putting together this mammoth document, however, begins a full year before the budget takes effect. At this time all the departments and state agencies begin to work on budget recommendations for the next fiscal year. For example, an agency starts working on its request for "FY 82" (the year beginning July 1, 1981) in the spring of 1980.

Department Hearings

First, under the state's open budget law, agencies must hold public hearings. At these hearings, the public can sometimes advise agencies of which programs should be funded and at what levels. Some agencies will use this input, but others will not. In some agencies, budget decisions are made before the public hearing, and the hearing is just a formality. Sometimes hearing testimony doesn't change the original agency request but will affect later proposals developed by the departmental secretaries, the Secretary of Administration and Finance, or the Governor. Sometimes testimony won't change anything. You can find out by talking to budget officers of each department. If a state election in the fall is likely to vote out the current administration and its recommendations, this may not be worth the time.

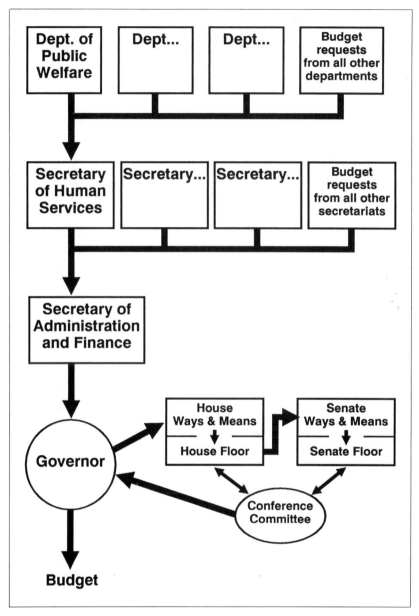

A chart showing the creation of the Massachusetts budget.

But, even if you expect no immediate response to your testimony, you should submit it in writing anyway. Later, when you lobby the W&M Committees, they will be more impressed with your group's hard work and knowhow if you can say that you testified to the agency and explain why your proposal was rejected. There is an increased respect for people who do their homework at each step.

To the Department Secretariat

The agency budget requests are then sent to the department secretary, who has another budget staff whose job is to approve or reduce each department budget. Department recommendations are frequently cut or eliminated—but rarely expanded.

To Administration and Finance

From the departmental secretary's office, the budget goes to the Office of Administration and Finance (A&F). This secretariat is really the Governor's own budget staff; they examine the other nine secretaries' budgets to make sure that the total document reflects the Governor's political goals.

To the Governor

Finally A&F's recommendations are laid on the Governor's desk. The Secretary of A&F and the Governor spend the Christmas and New Year's holidays meeting with secretariat heads, department heads, and outside special interest groups to make last-minute changes in the budget before it goes to the printers.

The Governor must submit this budget to the state legislature within three weeks after it convenes in January. A newly elected administration can submit the budget bill within seven weeks. The budget is always numbered **House 1,** and it must contain all proposed expenditures for the coming fiscal year.

The Legislative Branch: Out of the Frying Pan, into the Fire

According to the Massachusetts Constitution, all appropriation and taxation bills must originate in the House, and so the Governor files his budget with the House Clerk, who refers it to House Ways and Means. House 1 usually consists of three or four thick volumes narrating the line items and highlighting new initiatives. The House, and later the Senate, Ways and Means Committees are the central bodies for legislative consideration of the budget.

First the House W&M Committee reviews the Governor's budget, holds public hearings to interview department and agency staff, develops its own version of the budget, and reports that version out to the floor where it is debated and amended, line item by line item. Senate Ways and Means does not wait until the House has finished debating the budget to begin its own analysis of House 1, but must hold off reporting out its version to the Senate floor until the House is finished.

Since the House and Senate versions of the budget are often drastically different, the inevitable conference committee reports out a compromise version to the House and Senate for approval. The budget then goes to the Governor's desk, where individual line items may be reduced or amended or vetoed, while he signs the rest into law.

That is the budget process in a nutshell; the next pages describe the process in more detail.

The House

House W&M Hearings. The House W&M Committee analyzes the budget and holds public hearings. Unlike the joint committees, the W&M Committee only takes testimony from the state bureaucracy—cabinet secretaries, commissioners, department heads, and their staff.

After these hearings, W&M holds a final public hearing at which the public *can* testify on any portion of the budget. After all this, House W&M writes a budget and reports it to the full House by the second Wednesday in May. Under House rules, it must be in print at least seven days before the day scheduled for House action. This rule can, of course, be suspended.

House Version. But what does this famous budget bill actually look like at this point? First, it includes a total figure for anticipated state spending that year. *Section 1* is a paragraph authorizing the expenditure of funds. *Section 2* contains almost 2000 separate **line item appropriations**—that is, the dollar amounts to be spent by individual agencies for certain programs.

It also contains **outside sections**—limitations, restrictions, or conditions under which funds can be spent. In the past, many of these outside sections were separate bills tacked onto the budget by W&M because they addressed controversial issues which would have trouble passing any other way. Recent legislation has restricted the use of outside sections; now they include only language which directly affects particular line items.

House Floor Action. On the House floor, the budget follows the same procedure as any other bill—second reading, third read-

reimbursements received by the department shall be credited to the General Fund; including not more than two hundred positions   7,825,221

4800-0020   For the delivery of permanency services to children in the care of the department, including the provision of adoption, guardianship and subsidies; provided that the department shall make assessment of all the children in its care longer than twelve months for the appropriateness of adoption; provided further, that the department shall maintain a central registry and tracking system to monitor the progress of such children in the adoption process; and provided further, that no funds shall be expended to provide subsidies to adoptive parents for children no longer in their care; including not more than twenty-nine positions   20,216,936

4800-0023   For programs of adolescent assessment and treatment   2,802,685

4800-0025   For a program of foster care review, including not more than sixty-two positions   2,271,285

4800-0030   For the delivery of foster care services to children in the care of the department, including the provision of foster care subsidies, services to foster families, and reimbursements to foster parents for extraordinary expenses incurred ...   46,615,589

4800-0050   For the expenses and operations of the New Chardon Street Home for Women located in the city of Boston, including not more than twenty-one positions   599,075

4800-0060   For a program of day care services; provided, that vacant contracted basic slots will be filled through an alternating intake system, monitored by the department of social services, provided further, that any federal reimbursement for this purpose, unless otherwise authorized to be expended, shall be credited to the General Fund; provided further, that any participating voucher provider with fifty or more voucher placements, where said placements constitute fifty or more per cent of the provider's total program capacity, shall submit a proposal for contracted day care, and enter into contract negotiations with the department of social services; and provided further, that failure to enter into a contract for day care shall require that the provider limit voucher enrollment to fewer than fifty children, where said enrollments constitute fifty or more per cent of the provider's total program capacity; provided, that any voucher provider with fifty or more voucher placements, where said placements constitute fifty or more per cent of the provider's total program capacity, who has been denied a day care contract with the department of social services, shall not enter into a voucher provider agreement without sign-off by the commissioner of the department of social services including, for the voucher day care program, not more than nine positions   102,530,209

4800-0100   For the administration of the department's six regions, including not more than five hundred and eighty-five positions   25,395,650

A page from the House budget with a lobbyist's notes from the floor debate in the margins.

ing, engrossment, and enactment. Amendments are offered and debated, often at great length. Budget debates in the House have taken two weeks of round-the-clock sessions. After the budget is passed to be engrossed in the House, the Senate gets a crack at it.

The Senate

The procedure in the Senate is very similar to that in the House. One might assume that the Senate would carefully examine the House W&M report and the amendments added to it during debate as a guidepost. But it doesn't. The Senate virtually rewrites the whole thing, substituting its own version for the House bill.

Senate W&M Hearings. First, the Clerk refers the budget to Senate W&M, which holds another set of public hearings with the heads of departments and secretariats. These are followed by one public hearing for people on the outside. Recently these hearings have been held before the House has finished its debate on the budget.

There is no deadline for the Senate W&M Committee to report out the budget—except for the practical deadline of July 1st when the prior fiscal year ends. If it hasn't passed by then, the state will be without funds, and, there will be no pay for state employees and for state programs. Public pressure generally forces them, therefore, to act within a reasonable time.

Senate Version. The Senate W&M budget shows, for each department or program, (1) the previous year's appropriation; (2) the Governor's recommendation; (3) the final House recommendation; and (4) the Senate Committee on Ways and Means recommendation.

The bill must be in print and available to the members of the Senate at least five days before floor action is scheduled. Like most other rules, this one can be suspended at the leadership's whim or when or when a crisis demands it. Information is power. When the leadership plans to severely cut or increase controversial programs, its direct self-interest lies in giving opponents little time or information for lobbying.

Senate Floor Action. Senate floor action on the budget is similar to House action, except for one Senate rule: If anyone offers a budget amendment after the second or third reading of the budget, the vote on this amendment can be postponed until the next day at the request of two members of the Senate and must be printed in the calendar for the next day. Recently the Senate budget debate has lasted two days at the most.

Technically, once passed to be engrossed, the Senate bill goes to the House for concurrence (agreement with content). Of course, the House never concurs, so a conference committee is appointed.

ITEM NO.	TOTAL '88 APR.	GOVERNOR (REVISED)	HOUSE: FINAL ACTION		SENATE: WAYS AND MEANS RECOMMENDATION	
			DEPARTMENT OF PUBLIC HEALTH.		**DEPARTMENT OF PUBLIC HEALTH.**	
4510-0100	5,645,000	5,904,380	The department of public health shall submit quarterly to the house and senate committees on ways and means a status report on all public health hospitals, by individual hospital, including, but not limited to, inpatient and outpatient utilization, costs, revenues, personnel, contract expenditures, and capacity by service and use of such facilities by other state agencies and vendor programs.		The department of public health shall submit quarterly to the house and senate committees on ways and means a status report on all public health hospitals, by individual hospital, including, but not limited to, inpatient and outpatient utilization, costs, revenues, personnel, contract expenditures, and capacity by service and use of such facilities by other state agencies and vendor programs.	3,798,432
			For the administration of the department including a long term care information system for the state medicaid program; provided, that the position of assistant commissioner shall not be subject to chapter thirty-one of the General Laws, including not more than one hundred and six positions	6,670,059	For the administration of the department including a long term care information system for the state medicaid program; provided, that the position of assistant commissioner shall not be subject to chapter thirty-one of the General Laws, including not more than one hundred and six positions	
4510-0101	—	—	For a reserve to meet personnel costs of the department; provided, that funds may be transferred to other items of appropriation, provided further, that the department shall notify the house and senate committees on ways and means of all transfers made from this item	69,087		
4510-0102	916,984	562,275	For the administration of the division of environmental epidemiology and toxicology, including not more than fifteen positions	562,275		
4510-0103	862,831	770,506	For the administration of the division of health promotion; provided, that not less than sixty-five thousand dollars be expended for the Governor's Committee on Physical Fitness and Sports, including not more than fifteen positions	946,270		
4510-0106	—	—			For the rental costs of the Department; provided, that all of the rental obligations incurred by the Department shall be met from this line item and no other line items may be assessed such obligations	
4510-0110	1,649,228	1,659,793	For community and other health centers operational grants program; provided, that the department of public health shall solicit grant proposals for said operational grants from community health centers which are operating under the requirements of section three hundred and thirty of Public Law 95-626, as most recently amended by Public Law 97-35, and shall establish appropriate standards and criteria for the awarding of not less than one million four hundred thousand dollars in grant funds; provided further, that one hundred thousand dollars shall be obligated to establish a diabetes outreach program for the elderly and inner city population of the central area of the commonwealth; and provided further, that		For community and other health centers operational grants program; provided, that the department of public health shall solicit grant proposals for said operational grants from community health centers which are operating under the requirement of section three hundred and thirty of Public Law 95-626, as most recently amended by Public Law 97-35, and shall establish appropriate standards and criteria for the awarding of not less than one million four hundred thousand dollars in grant funds; provided further, that not less than one hundred and twenty-five thousand dollars shall be obligated for the Dimock Community Health Center; provided further, that notwithstanding the provisions of any general or	2,981,090

A page from the Senate budget with a lobbyist's notes from the conference committee in the margins.

Conference Committees

Composition.   The conference committee has traditionally been composed of the chairs and vice-chairs of the House and Senate W&M Committees and one minority (Republican) member of each of the Committees. All are appointed by the Speaker and the Senate President. The public meetings of the conference committee are always packed with members of the press, representatives from the Governor's office, and advocacy groups. The real decisions, however, are usually made in private meetings between the Speaker, the Senate President, the W&M chairs, and whomever else they care to include.

Function.   The conference committee works only on line items in which the House and Senate versions conflict in the language or dollar amounts appropriated, or both. These items are said to be "subject to conference." For example, the committee can either choose the House or the Senate version intact or they can agree to "split the difference." If they do the latter, they must come up with something between the two versions. In the example above, they might choose to establish eight positions and to appropriate $100,000.

Finally, the committee can and does often mutually agree to amend some line items by inserting entirely new, but related language. In this way, just six members of the legislature can (by changing a word or two) redirect state policy and programs. For instance, imagine that a phrase were added to the fuel assistance account which permitted small oil dealers to be paid up front for oil delivered to welfare recipients instead of having to wait 90 days for payment. Many more of them would be willing to deliver oil to low-income households.

Floor Action Again.   After the conference committee has forged a bill which four of its members will sign, this **conference committee report** is passed to be engrossed—first in the House, then in the Senate. If it fails in either house, the bill returns to the conference committee, which must try again. Although they call it a new conference committee, actually the same members are appointed. After both branches accept the conference committee's report, the bill goes to the Governor for signature.

Back to the Executive Branch: the Governor's Desk

The Governor can act on the budget as he can on any other bill—with one major exception. With other bills, the Governor must sign or veto the whole bill. But in the budget the Governor can veto or reduce individual line items (those contained in Section 2 of the budget) and approve the rest of it. Usually, the Governor vetoes some outside sections, vetoes or reduces the line items he opposes, and signs the rest into law. The rejected or reduced items are then subject to the same procedure as any other vetoed bill. A 2/3 vote is required in each house to override the Governor's veto.

Lobbying the Budget Process

The arena is smaller, the timeframe is shorter, but the same rules apply: Decision makers make different decisions when watched by the affected constituents; get the right information to the right people at the right time.

First review the budget and identify all the line items and outside sections that apply to your issue. Second, identify the individual staff people in both W&M committees who are assigned to analyze those items and sections. Third, prepare detailed backup material to support any changes you want and submit them to the staff of both committees. (Don't even think about playing one staff committee person off against the other; they talk to each other all the time.) Third, identify a list of legislators who will champion your budget requests with the W&M Committees. If possible you want your changes inserted in the W&M version; if necessary, you want your champions to amend the budget on the floor.

Sounds easy. But what if something goes wrong? (It will.)

Review the Budget Closely

Perhaps only a handful of people in the State House actually pretend to understand the destination of each tax dollar and the public policy behind each line item. You don't have to be one of them. Just understand the line items pertinent to *your* programs, and make sure your organization and individual legislators understand them, too.

To aid this education process, write and distribute a simple narrative explaining the impact of each relevant line item and outside section on your group's members or programs affecting them— both the favorable and unfavorable ones—and include your group's recommendations for change.

Working with Staff

Ask for meetings with the appropriate budget analysts in the department, the Secretariat, and the W&M Committees. If possible, schedule these meetings during the time each group is actively working on the budget. That means meeting with department people in the summer, secretariat people in the fall, House W&M people in the winter, and Senate W&M people in the spring. It's better to meet with department and secretariat people late rather than never. If they say they're too busy to discuss it with you, send them your budget narrative anyway. If you run into trouble getting a meeting with W&M people, a request from a friendly legislator on your behalf may work.

At these meetings, share all the data you have supporting your recommendations. Most department budget staff, you will find, welcome any support for increasing their own department's budget. Secretariat and W&M budget staffs, on the other hand, are more interested in keeping costs down. All of them, however, are suitably impressed and sometimes intimidated by advocacy groups with good, accurate information.

Working with Legislators

Using the same data and information on your line items and outside sections, find legislators who will be your budget advocates the same way you looked for sponsors on other bills. The most likely prospects are the members of the committees which review your issue. A local legislator is the best person to champion a local problem. Once the legislator understands exactly how the line item or outside section should be amended or protected, he or she must deliver that message and its importance to the leadership and the chairs of W&M.

This is another good spot to insert your legislative network into the process. By writing letters, they can apply heat to their own representatives and senators, the leadership, and the chairs of W&M. Their message should be a simple one, such as, "Restore full funding to H.5406 to keep the handicapped children in our area in school."

Sometimes your legislator budget advocate and all your letters fail to convince the leadership to amend your line item in the W&M report. In this case, ask your supporting legislator to propose an amendment during floor debate. If he or she agrees, you must help him or her manage a floor fight. Draft the amendment, identify a floor team, and lobby the entire membership exactly as outlined in Chapter 5.

Budget floor fights differ from regular debates and roll calls in one respect: There is even more leadership investment and control. The budget document embodies a statement of leadership's view of how the state government should run. Leadership is invested personally and politically in preventing any major erosions or additions to the legislation. In return for maintaining the general parameters of the budget, they will often permit individual legislators to insert minor amendments.

Your job, then, is two-pronged. On one hand, you must convince the leadership that your amendment makes only a minor change within the context of the whole budget. At the same time, you must persuade your supporters that this amendment is enormously important—so important that if the leadership opposes it, these members will threaten to break ranks and vote against adoption of the budget as a whole. It's not as tricky as it sounds. The leadership expects negotiations, and the rank-and-file members enjoy an opportunity to bargain. Recent House budget debates have actually recessed while leadership negotiated with rebellious members fighting to restore a wide range of services.

The Conference Committee

You have been tracking the budget for six months. The Governor underfunded your program, but House W&M restored part of the money. Your organization and your House supporters were unable to convince the leadership to insert the rest. However, the Speaker said if you could get the money fully restored in the Senate, House leadership might instruct the House conference committee members to accept the Senate version of your line item. Subsequently, you succeeded in getting your item fully restored in the Senate.

Now you are sitting in a small room packed with press, bureaucrats, and other advocacy groups. You can barely hear the chair of Senate W&M reading a series of line item numbers and saying, "The Senate recedes," which means they yield to the House version. Sometimes the chair of House W&M inserts, "The House recedes." Occasionally one or the other stops to confer with the budget analyst sitting beside him and requests a "hold on that item, please." They go on and on.

Eventually you notice that the budget analysts you met with from both House and Senate W&M have moved into place beside their respective chairmen, and you hear numbers of the line items within the department administering your program. You perk up, strain to hear and, at last, the Senate chair reads your line item number. After what seems an excruciatingly long conference with the budget staff person, the House chair of W&M announces, "The House recedes." It happened right in front of your eyes!

It happened, all right, but not actually before your eyes. The real decision was made in a series of prior private conversations be-

A conference committee splitting the difference.

tween the Speaker, the Senate President, the chairs of W&M, and appropriate staff. The public conference committee meetings are really just public announcements of these decisions.

Nevertheless, it's important to be there. You can be sure that your hard work briefing legislators, distributing fact sheets, and organizing letter-writing campaigns was noticed, as is your presence at the annual conference committee vigil. The final conversation in the leadership meeting probably went something like this:

Senate President: Well, what'dya want to do about this one? We think the program's a good one, and the parent group really wants it.

Speaker: I know, they've been everywhere. We're not crazy about it, but a bunch of my guys love it, and I've been getting heat from all over the state. What are the numbers?

Staff: It's only $800,000 and it'll mean 300 more handicapped kids get into the program.

Speaker: OK. We'll go with the Senate numbers. Tell those parents they can stop calling and go home.

The amount of lobbying work behind that fleeting conversation should be evident by now. *But the last thing the parent group should do is go home.*

The Governor

Preventing a Veto or Reduction.   Your budget item is not law yet—not until it is approved (or not disapproved) by the Governor. Your final job is making sure the Governor does not veto or reduce your line item or outside section.

Previous work with departmental and secretariat budget staff will come in handy now. They are the ones to whom the Governor will turn for recommendations on the budget. It's important to touch base with them now to find out if he's even considering a veto or reduction.

Regardless of whether the Governor is thinking of scrapping your budget item, this is the time to pump messages to him from all your supporters and allies including legislators. The Governor must sign the parts of the budget he approves within ten days, so you haven't got much time.

If You're Vetoed.   The Governor sends all budget vetoes and line item reductions to the House Clerk in one "Message from his Excellency"; then the whole package is sent to House W&M. Ways and Means, however, reports out each line item veto or reduction separately and usually reports out only those items the leadership supports. If 2/3 of the House members vote to override a veto or line item reduction, each one is sent separately to the Senate. The items that win a 2/3 majority to override in the Senate are then restored to the total budget, despite the Governor's disapproval.

Lobbying to override the Governor's budget vetoes is the same as lobbying to override any other veto. (See Chapter 6 section on overriding the Governor.)

Other Appropriations Acts

Sometimes the legislature, like the rest of us, finds that it has budgeted inadequately for the whole year or wants to keep some accounts separate from the rest of the budget. To deal with these situations, either supplemental or deficiency budgets must be passed.

Supplemental Budgets

Supplemental budgets fund two kinds of programs: (1) new ones created by the legislature; and (2) programs underfunded in the main budget. These appropriations, like the main budget, must be filed by the Governor. They can be enacted *only after* passage of the general appropriations act.

Deficiency Budgets

A deficiency budget is passed if a state agency or program has spent all its funds before the end of the fiscal year and needs more. Special interest groups often lobby for deficiency and supplemental budgets if they include funds for programs the group supports. Even if a supplemental or deficiency budget submitted by the Governor does not include such items, the legislature can add them in committee or on the floor.

Special Appropriations

Special appropriations are those which the legislature initiates after the state budget has been enacted. All appropriations were done this way until the reform movement of the early 1900s put all appropriations into a general appropriation act. Now special appropriations are seldom enacted.

All these appropriation acts follow the same legislative paths as the general appropriations bill. Trying to influence them is also the same.

Fractional Budgets

Sometimes the legislature does not pass a budget by the July 1st deadline. Usually, they simply keep trying and pass it when agreement is reached. But until then, the state has no operating funds. Agency bills go unpaid, and state employees and welfare recipients receive no checks. The longer this situation exists, the greater the pressure on the legislature to do something. If serious differences remain, rather than be pressured into unwanted compromises, the legislature may pass a fractional budget to keep the government financially afloat until the whole budget is approved.

A fractional budget appropriates the minimum amount of funds needed to keep state operations intact for one to three months. The current cost of operations for a full year is divided by whatever fraction is desired—1/12 for one month, 2/12 for two months, and so on. No new programs or increased expenditures are included. The fractional budget is simply a stopgap.

Other Kinds of Bills Referred to Ways and Means

Why Bills Are Referred to Ways and Means

Bills must be referred to the W&M Committees if they:

- involve public money;
- involve a grant of federal money, or
- otherwise affect state finances.

Ways and Means must review each bill's cost and impact on state finances. In addition, bills costing more than $100,000 must have **fiscal notes** attached to them when reported out of W&M. The fiscal note states how much public money would be spent to carry out the bill's provisions. If the bill sets up a new program, the note includes an estimated first year cost.

Except for the fiscal note, bills reported out of W&M follow the same legislative course as bills reported out of any joint committee.

However, bills are also sent to W&M, not for financial review, but to delay or kill them. Because almost any bill affects state finances, it's easy for a bill's opponents to ship the unwanted bill to these committees. While in W&M, the bill no longer appears on the calendar. Out of sight, out of mind. And, conveniently, W&M has no deadlines for reporting bills out. (Technically, House W&M must report on all bills referred to it, but there's no deadline, so the rule has no teeth.) (Getting bills out of W&M is discussed later in this chapter.)

Routes to W&M

From Joint Committees.   Almost all bills go to a joint committee for review before going to W&M. Unlike the budget bill, which must be sent to House W&M, joint committees can send bills to the W&M Committee of either branch. In most cases, however, the joint committee sends House bills to House W&M and Senate bills to Senate W&M. A good lobbyist will ask that a bill be sent to the friendliest W&M committee.

Sometimes, a bill is sent to W&M in one branch, goes through its three readings and is never sent to W&M in the other branch. Occasionally, bills which should be referred to W&M are not. Both incidents are usually oversights. If no one objects, the bills may simply go on their way.

Money Bills.   But there is one exception to the rule of allowing bills to go to either W&M Committee—**money bills.** Money bills are those which provide for raising the funds necessary to pay for new or increased expenditures. These bills usually come out of the Committees on Taxation, Counties, or Local Affairs, and deal with plans for raising state, county, and local taxes, respectively. Money bills must be sent to the House, where they are referred to House W&M. Then, they follow the same path as any other W&M bill.

Also, nonmoney bills are sometimes amended at second and third reading to become money bills, and then go to House W&M. For instance, a bill expanding state scholarships may be amended to include a raise in cigarette taxes to fund this increased cost to the state. If there is any doubt about whether a bill should go to W&M, it usually goes.

Getting a Bill Out of W&M

Getting a bill *into* W&M is often easier than getting it *out*, but there are ways and means to do so. First, find out why it was sent there—for serious review of its cost and impact on state finances, or just to bury it for the session. If it was sent there for serious review, facts and figures can sometimes dislodge it. If it was sent there to kill it, you will need political muscle to rescue it. Usually it's a combination of the two; and the combination varies from branch to branch, depending on the personal quirks of the leadership and the W&M chairs.

Facts and Figures

If the chair is concerned about the cost of the bill, you can calm that fear. Show him or her figures illustrating how minimal the cost really is, how much money will be saved in the long run, or how many safeguards against big spending abuses are already written into the bill. The chair will give your bill a favorable report only if he or she has facts and figures to support the decision during floor debate. Also, the chair will want to know that your floor team is ready to carry the burden of debate, because dissidents and minority party members will surely be lying in wait to cross-examine the W&M chair on program costs. Make sure whoever is on your side gets the information they need in time for these fights.

Political Muscle

Unlike the budget, which must be passed in some form by the beginning of the fiscal year, other bills sent to W&M have no deadline and can get bogged down there. But certain people can push them up and out. They are:

- leadership (Speaker, President, and assistants);
- W&M chairs;
- other committee chairs;
- W&M staff;
- a close friend of the W&M chair;
- one or several W&M committee members;
- several members of the legislature;
- voting constituents in the chair's district; and
- the media.

Sometimes, all of the above must be used.

Remember—there are two distinct W&M Committees. Although disagreement between the two committees over the budget must be resolved, disagreement over a particular bill can remain unsolved indefinitely. Unless someone pushes, and pushes *hard,* a bill can sit in one W&M Committee, despite support from the chair of the other one. In these situations, tacking a bill onto the budget as an outside section is a good way to push it into the arena where the legislature must act on it.

But unless you have enough votes on the floor to pass the bill, leave it in W&M. Why waste time in a futile effort to rescue a bill only to have it killed on the floor? Lobby the membership instead. Often the leadership claims, "The votes aren't there," when no one really knows. Do your own vote count. When you have floor support, use it to persuade the W&M chair to release your bill.

Discharge Procedures

When nothing else works, bills can be forced out of either W&M Committee by a motion to discharge. A bill must be reported out of

Senate W&M when a majority of the members of W&M submit a specific request in writing to the chairperson. A motion from the floor must be printed on the calendar. A two-thirds vote of the members present and voting is required if the bill has been in W&M for less than 45 days, and a majority vote if the bill has been in W&M for more than 45 days. A motion to discharge a bill from House W&M must sit on the calendar for 7 legislative days, but only takes a majority vote.

The Other Side of the Coin: Keeping a Bill Bottled Up

In all legislative action, it's easier to stop a bill than to push one forward. The Committees on W&M are not exceptions. It's easier to bottle up a bill there than to release one.

If the W&M committee chair does not object, you can simply send an opponent's bill there to disappear. To do this, get cooperation from the appropriate joint committee chair, the Clerk, the President, or the Speaker.

This tactic can also be used to slow down your own bills when necessary. Sometimes you will need time to analyze a bill, to iron out compromises, or to mobilize support. Sending a bill to W&M is one way to buy that time.

Chapter 8

USING THE MEDIA IN A LEGISLATIVE CAMPAIGN

by Linda Myer

Why Use the Media in a Legislative Campaign?

The basic premise of public interest group lobbying is that legislators make different decisions when watched by affected constituents. Legislators who know that voters are watching will often vote to please them.

The mass media are tools for convincing legislators that their actions are being watched—not only by people in the gallery, but also by countless others reading the papers, listening to radio, or watching television. The media can give all your other lobbying efforts more "oomph." For example, if your group calls a press conference before a committee hearing and reporters attend, the committee members will listen more carefully to the discussions about your bill at the hearing itself.

The other important use of media in your campaign is to increase the grassroots support for your bill. In the example above, you'll need a big public turnout at the committee hearing to impress the committee members. To get that support, you must build public concern about your issue in the press. Before the hearing, try to get stories about the bill into the newspapers; these stories should explain why the bill is important and to whom.

These two functions—showing legislators their decisions will be watched by affected constituents and building grassroots support—operate together. The more concerned citizens you have in the network, the more attention you'll get in the press and from legisla-

The mass media are tools for convincing legislators that their actions are being watched.

tors. Greater media and legislative attention will, in turn, attract more grassroots interest in your issue.

This chapter describes how to use the media to achieve both goals in your lobbying campaign. Coordinating all the media events in your campaign is a big job—too big to be done by your group's lobbyist who coordinates between the state legislature and the grassroots network, the **media planner** coordinates between the press, the lobbyist, and the network.

The media planner and the lobbyist must be a close duo, because teamwork between them is essential. The lobbyists therefore must tell the media planner what's happening to the bill, what kind of media pressure will be useful, and when to set it in action. As the lobbyist becomes the spokesperson for the bill in the legislature, the media planner becomes your group's spokesperson for the press. Accordingly, the media person must know what the bill does and how it will help the affected constituency. Here again, sharing all information between the lobbyist and the media planner is crucial to your group presenting a clear, strong image in the public eye.

Public or Nonpublic Issue?

The first question in a publicity campaign for a bill is, "What kind of publicity will you need to pass the legislation?" The answer depends largely on whether the bill addresses a public or a nonpublic issue.

Public Issues

Of the thousands of bills introduced in each legislative session, only a handful address **public issues.** Is your bill one of these?

Your bill is a public issue if almost everyone (1) has heard of it, (2) knows it's being debated in the legislature, (3) has an opinion on it, and (4) knows who the players are on each side. Recent examples of public issues in Massachusetts are the Bottle Bill, which requires beer and soft drink containers to carry deposit charges, and Proposition 2-1/2, which limits annual increases in property taxes to 2-1/2 percent of the previous year's valuation.

Nonpublic Issues

About 90 percent of the bills in the legislature address **nonpublic issues.** These issues, though quite painful and important to those directly affected by them, are generally unknown to everyone else. Only the people suffering under the current law, their advocates, concerned legislators, the bill's sponsors, and administrators of state programs related to the problem will follow the progress of these bills. Examples of nonpublic issue bills include those which clarify the rights of handicapped persons, establish environmental programs affecting only particular communities, or simplify procedures in government programs.

Don't assume that bigger is always better in the game of passing legislation. Working on big public issues appears glamorous, but these fights are often the hardest to win because the opposition mobilizes so forcefully against them. (The old law of Newtonian physics: To every action there is an equal and opposite reaction.) Often it's easier to succeed in lobbying for bills addressing nonpublic issues. If you keep quiet, these bills may arouse no opposition and will pass unnoticed.

Because nonpublic issues are better left quiet and because public issues are already widely publicized, media strategy for these two kinds of bills differs. Later in this chapter, both types of strategy are described in detail.

Who Are the Media?

Before describing a publicity campaign, let's define some terms about "the media."

Mass Media and Other Kinds

There are countless kinds of media which give us messages every day. In addition to the **mass media** (newspapers, radio, and television), there are also billboards, posters, campaign buttons, T-shirts, slide shows, and leaflets. You can use all of these in publicizing your bill. Many of the nonmass media are used to build your grassroots network rather than to convince legislators to vote for your bill.

This chapter, however, will deal specifically with using the mass media. There are two reasons for this emphasis: (1) people new to legislative campaigns often are overwhelmed by the mass media and need some tips; and (2) there are other, more complete sources for planning leaflets, posters, and other organizing tools.

Local Press and State House Press

Here we'll focus on using newspapers, radio, and television—or, what is conveniently called **the press.** But the press can be broken down into parts, too. The most important distinction for media planners is between the local press and the legislative press corps. In Massachusetts, there are reporters who cover the State House exclusively. In other states, this function may not be a full-time job, but there will be someone regularly assigned to cover the state legislature from each news outlet.

The Local Press.   The **local press** includes local newspapers and magazines, local radio stations, and some local television stations, especially those on cable TV. Legislators use local press outlets extensively to tap into public opinion in their home districts. So publicity in the local press is crucial to garnering legislative votes for your bill.

The State House Press Corps.   These are the men and women hanging around the corridors of the state capitol covering all relevant stories for their respective news outlets. In Massachusetts, the corps includes reporters from the Boston newspapers, other large-city papers in Massachusetts, radio stations, television stations, and wire services. Usually, they cover several select stories repeatedly; sometimes it's difficult to get their attention for any other issues. Generally, they are in a big hurry.

Media Strategies for Nonpublic Issues

Even though nonpublic issues are often most successful when kept out of the public's eye, they still need some publicity. But they need a different kind of publicity with different goals.

Objectives

A media strategy for nonpublic issues has two main goals: (1) convincing local legislators that large numbers of the constituents affected by your bill live in her or his district and are watching what she or he does; and (2) recruiting more of those affected constituents into your network.

Use Local Media Extensively

Your main goal in lobbying for a nonpublic issue is to convince individual legislators that their own constituents are affected by the problem. Legislators look to the local media for information about their constituents' views, so the main thrust of your media campaign for nonpublic issues will be in the local press. The best strategy is to give local legislators the opportunity to look like heroes in their own districts by supporting a bill that their own voters favor. Here are some ways to do it.

- Call a meeting in the district on the issue. Invite the legislator and other local bigwigs to address the meeting and get your local reporters to attend.
- When the legislator does something to help the bill through the legislature, send press releases to all local news media describing the member's actions.
- Invite the member to appear with you on local talk shows to answer citizens' questions and to hear their comments on the issue.
- When something happens that's directly related to the problem the bill addresses, get the local papers to write features about it. Also, people in your network should write letters to the editor about the issue. Or try to convince the local paper to let your group submit an **op-ed piece** (opinion essay) for the editorial page.

All these activities show the legislators that people in the district care about the bill. But they keep the focus local so that the statewide news outlets and your opponents hear very little about it. Also the meetings, talk shows, and articles will build up local interest on the issue by educating local constituents about the effects of the bill on them and on their own legislator's view on the issue.

Keeping your group's name in the local press will also enhance grassroots support for your organization. People will see that *you* are the ones trying to do something about this issue. Make sure your group's name, address, and phone number appear in stories and announcements so that people can call you for more information or offer their services or financial support.

Using the State House Press Corps

Most of your media work for nonpublic issues will be with local press outlets—but not all. When something significant happens to your bill in the legislature—such as passage from one branch to the other, or a favorable report out of W&M—you may want the State House press to cover it. If so, distribute a press release to all members of the press corps. This release should include the names of the bill's sponsors, a description of what the bill will do, and an account of where the bill will go next in the legislative process. (More on distributing press releases later in this chapter.)

Another tactic is to get a feature story related to the bill into the news. Reporters often couple human interest stories with the drier accounts of voting results and committee reports. Let's assume your bill proposes a change in zoning laws which will make it easier to establish group homes for retarded adults. And suppose you know of a home where the retarded residents were absorbed smoothly into the neighborhood. Suggest a feature about this success story to a friendly reporter.

If you get this kind of coverage from them, terrific! If not, don't worry about it. Put most of your time and energy into the local media campaign. That's the fastest, most certain way to get the votes needed to pass your nonpublic issue bill.

Public Issue Publicity Strategy

Publicity campaigns for public issue bills have somewhat different goals. Legislators will already know something about these issues and be aware that some people in their districts are affected and concerned. In fact, on these issues, just about everyone is watching. So what is the purpose of publicity in this kind of campaign?

Your publicity goals are: (1) to maintain your group's position as a forceful player in the decision-making process—a player to be reckoned with; and (2) to build more grassroots support both for the issue and for your group. To accomplish these goals, use the local press as described above to pressure particular legislators to vote for your bill.

But your work with the State House press corps will be different. These issues form the bulk of the State House reporters' work. Whenever something happens—a bill is reported out of committee or passes in one branch or the other—reporters describe the events and then search for comments by representatives of opposing factions to spice up their stories with controversy. Your goal is to become one of their "quotable sources," someone they can count on for a good one-liner on your group's attitude toward that day's event. Being a quotable source keeps your group's name and opinions in the news; and keeping your group in the public eye will, in turn, strengthen your position inside the state legislature and among potential grassroots supporters.

To become a quotable source, you must be articulate and available. Prepare in advance a two- or three-sentence reaction to the news. Be there when the news breaks, and *tell reporters you are there.* If you can't be there, tell the group's lobbyists or the bill's sponsor where you can be reached for a comment. And be there! Once you develop good rapport with the press, they will call you immediately for statements.

Mechanics of Working with the State House Press

Knowing which reporters to approach and how to do so may seem overwhelming to a novice. But isn't hard when you learn the mechanics.

Where to Find Them

In the Massachusetts State House there are four designated press rooms. One room houses *Boston Globe* reporters; in another are reporters from the *Boston Herald,* other large city newspapers, and the wire services. A third is for the State House news service, which sends information to small press outlets lacking Boston correspondents, to state government offices, and to anyone else who wants it. The fourth room lodges the broadcast reporters, both radio and television.

Tools for Getting Their Attention

There are three main tools for getting the State House press to notice something: the press release, the news conference, and the report.

Press Releases. The **press release** is the general currency of the news world. It is the accepted form of communication from newsmakers to news reporters.

Whenever something significant happens to your bill, draft a press release about it and distribute about 100 copies in the four press rooms. In the State House news service room, there are boxes for each reporter; plug one into each box. In the other rooms, distribute them to each desk and leave a pile in a central location.

Send a release before all important votes on your bill, and send
another reporting the results afterward. Press releases should be
short, and factual, and should include names and phone numbers of
people to contact for more information. (More on writing press
releases later in this chapter.)

News Conferences.   News conferences keep your group's name
and views in the public's eye even when nothing much is happening to your bill at the State House. Sometimes organizers suggest
holding news conferences out in the community to draw more local
people, but this will radically decrease coverage by the State
House press. If the latter is your goal, hold the conference in the
State House.

There are many good opportunities for news conferences. For
example, if your opposition has held one, you can schedule one the
following day to refute their allegations. Any new development is a
good excuse for a news conference. You can announce events both
within the legislature (for example, the bill passed out of committee; or a maverick group of senators will oppose the leadership to
support the bill) or outside of it (for example, a judge has just ruled
on something which makes your bill essential to correct the injus-
tice, or a new group of people have been harmed by the current
law). If there's been a disaster related to issues your bill addresses,
a news conference can make the connection clearer. If a study
about the problems your bill addresses has just been completed,
publicize its release with the fanfare of a news conference.

O.K., so you're holding a news conference. How do you go about
it? First, a legislator must request the room for you. Ask your bill's
sponsor or another supportive member to do so. Whoever requests
it must be present at the event.

Notify all members of the press corps by distributing a **press
advisory** the day before the news conference. Include the subject
of the conference, the names of speakers, the time, the date, the
place, and the names of contact persons for more information.
Distribute these just as you distribute press releases. For television
coverage, notify the assignment editor at each station so that he or
she can get the right people and equipment to the spot.

Both the press corps and television assignment editors should be
reminded again on the day of the news conference. Call the TV
assignment editors in the morning; warn the others an hour before,
either by phone or in person.

At the press conference, hand out a well-written press statement
including the basic information you hope to see in print. These
statements should be accurate and interesting. Include catchy
quotes and the names and positions of those quoted. Often big

portions of these prepared statements will appear on the news almost verbatim.

Reports and Studies. Distributing a report or study to the press is another great tactic for attracting coverage. Attach a press release to the report, stating its author, subject matter, and most significant findings. Studies backing up your position add weight to your opinions, thus increasing your credibility with legislators and the public.

Dealing with Reporters

In all your publicity activities, you will save your own and reporters' time—and will get much better coverage—by learning how to work with reporters. First, try to see the news and their job as they do. What are their functions and responsibilities? What kind of stories do they want? Understanding that, you can package your story so reporters will want to use it.

What Are Reporters Looking For?

A Newsworthy Story. Reporters are paid to report the news. But, what is news? Who decides which of the myriad events in a single day, in a single hour, are "news" and which are not. Part of the journalist's job is to decide which events are **newsworthy.** But what makes a story newsworthy?

Newspapers, magazines, radio, and television sell news as a product. So, what they publicize is usually a combination of what happens and what will sell papers or increase ratings. Here are some kinds of stories considered newsworthy.

Issues Affecting Large Numbers of People. Anything affecting most people in a given area will be automatically newsworthy in that area. Most public issues are big news topics week after week. Examples of these top-story issues are the Bottle Bill in Massachusetts, the federal budget, and the nuclear arms limitations talks.

Issues Heavily Affecting Specific Groups. Issues that don't affect most people may still be considered newsworthy in more specialized media outlets. For example, a story about a lake dying of pollution may not be reported nationally, but it might be a top story in the local papers near the lake and in nationally circulated environmentalist magazines.

Public Figures. The public and private lives of famous people— movie stars, politicians, athletes—are always news.

Heartstring Stories. Stories which tug on our emotions—

What do you have to do to get the press around here, anyway??

accidents, rape, lost children, fires, flood and pestilence—always attract attention.

"*Firsts.*" Unprecedented achievements (the first person on the moon) or the first member of a particular group to achieve something (the first woman Supreme Court justice) are sure to be reported.

Changes in Procedures and Trends. Similarly, events or laws overturning older traditions and practices are usually considered newsworthy. Studies revealing such changes—opinion polls and surveys of trends—also are good bets at making the news.

News Must Be New.   Reporters need a steady diet of *new* news. They can't sell today's papers with yesterday's headlines. In the news world, a big premium is placed on having the latest news, or on breaking a story before any competing news outlet does. That's part of what sells papers, and it's part of the sport of the profession.

Beats and Angles.   Big-city press staffs are divided into specific **beats,** such as the State House, courts, labor, education, and so on. Only the small outlets have general reporters who write everything from the editorials to the recipe column and weather reports.

Within these beats, reporters try to "slant" stories to interest their particular audiences. This direction of the story is called "giving it an angle." For example, all city papers in Massachusetts covered the issue of Proposition 2-1/2, the property tax-cutting referendum passed in 1981. But each paper slanted the story to show how Proposition 2-1/2 would affect the finances of its own city.

Journalists also use angles to freshen up old news. A major plane crash will stay in the paper at least a week, but reporters have to say something new each day. So, on successive days, they might write about a survivor's first-hand account, the rescue operation, and the investigation into causes of the crash.

Interesting Quotes.   Although news stories are supposed to be objective recountings of events, the public often wants to know what the different viewpoints are in a controversy. But instead of blatantly expressing their own opinions in news articles, news writers often quote other people who hold conflicting views on a topic or event.

Reporters also use quotes at the beginnings of stories to "hook" readers into reading or listening. A funny or dramatic quote in the first sentence grabs attention better than dry statements of fact.

How to Give Reporters the Stories They Need

Unless your bill addresses a big public issue, you'll have to package your story to attract press coverage. Following the points listed above, let's see how this is done with a hypothetical bill. Assume that you belong to a tenants' organization which is lobbying to pass a bill stopping condominium conversion in your city.

How to Make Your Issue Newsworthy.   This bill will directly affect many tenants, real estate developers, and prospective condo buyers all over the state. Even so, these groups may not be numerous enough to ensure automatic top-billing in the major news outlets.

Nonetheless, the issue can get good coverage. First, it will be a very newsworthy story in areas where many tenants have been, or will be, evicted due to heavy development by condo buyers. Neighborhood papers in these areas would be good markets for articles about the bill's progress in the legislature, letters to the editor from tenants facing eviction, and opinion pieces from your organization on the editorial page.

Second, you can get some coverage in the major media outlets by marketing your story cleverly. Do prominent people in the community publicly support the bill? Invite them to address your tenants' union and get some reporters to attend. Or, does a well-known political figure hold interest in the real estate companies doing the conversions? Reporters love stories exposing possible conflicts of interest in the lives of politicians.

This issue has lots of potential for heartstring-pulling feature stories. What will happen to the elderly tenants who must suddenly move? Where will they go? Have some of them set up a commune or become active in fighting the conversions?

Is the bill unique in some way? The first bill of its kind to be proposed in the state? The first tenants' organization in this area? Or the first legislation proposed by this tenant union? Perhaps this is the first issue which has melded a coalition of black and white tenants in this neighborhood. All are good stories.

If the bill passes, what changes will occur in the pattern of neighborhood development? Have any studies been done? If so, hold a news conference announcing the findings of the studies.

Keeping It Current.   Remember that reporters need *new* news every day. By keeping abreast of developments in the legislature and outside, you can forewarn reporters about newsworthy events, so they'll be ready and waiting when the story breaks. Learn each reporter's deadline time; it's useless to phone in information about today's events just before, or a little after, deadline.

How to Use Beats and Angles.   Figure out which writers cover your issue and stay in close touch, giving them frequent updates on the condo conversion bill. Also, occasionally try to get another reporter to cover it by pitching the story a different way. Talk to the real estate or business reporter about the effects of the bill on the rental housing market. Tell the City Hall writer about the effects of condo conversion on city voting patterns as new people move into older neighborhoods and replace the former voters.

Becoming a Quotable Source.   There will be times when nothing much is happening to your bill, but you want to keep the issue alive in the press anyway. Look around for events related to your bill. Perhaps your opponents have introduced a new bill providing special low-interest loans for condo developers; or a large area of rental housing will be razed to build a new shopping center, thus putting even more pressure on the already dwindling supply of rental units. Call up reporters, tell them who you represent, and offer your views on these events. If your information is interesting, accurate, and articulately presented, they may decide to write another story showing your side of the issue. If not, at least your opinion may be quoted in the original story. This alerts the public and legislators that you are still concerned about the issue. You could even mention the status of your bill in the legislature and get some free publicity.

Maintaining Good Working Relationships with Reporters

In addition to packaging your story in an appealing way, good press coverage also depends on maintaining good relationships with reporters. Once again, the reporter's job is to get the news out to the public as quickly and as accurately as possible. If you make the reporter's job easier, he or she will appreciate it and will keep coming back to you for more information. Your goal is to become a dependable "source."

Accuracy and Honesty.   Accuracy and honesty are the roots of any good relationship with reporters. As in dealing with legislators and their staffs, you have to give reporters accurate information if you want them to come back for more. It may be tempting to embellish what you know or to overstate things to make an impact. Resist this urge. Stick to what you know and what you can back up with statistics and other evidence. Reporters who write incorrect or misleading stories based on your information will suffer a loss of credibility in their trade—and they certainly won't ask for your help again.

If a journalist asks a question you can't answer, be honest about your ignorance. Then offer to find the information or suggest another source who can. If you offer to track down the answer, find out when the reporter needs it and get it to him or her promptly.

Clarity and Background Information.   When speaking to reporters, remember that you probably know much more about your issue than they do—even if they've been covering it for a while. Reporters are responsible for a wide variety of topics simultaneously; usually they don't get a chance to do much research on any one subject. Scrambling to keep up with daily events absorbs most of their time.

You can help them by presenting your facts clearly, logically, and slowly enough to be understood. Also, if you sense them hesitating in their questions, find out whether they are familiar with the situation you're discussing. If they aren't, fill them in on the details in a friendly way. You may have to provide background on the whole subject area; learn to present this history in a few brief concise sentences, because most reporters are pressed for time during interviews.

If the interview is planned in advance, send background information to the reporter beforehand. Again—be concise, clear, and accurate; they are more likely to read two pages than a hundred-page report. You can also include these information packets when you send press releases about current events. Reporters appreciate getting the information they need to ask the right questions.

Doing the Legwork.   News people appreciate anything you do that brings important information to their desks (or video display terminals, as is the case in many places now). Although recent movies and television series about journalists show them delving deeply into one particular big story, few work this way in real life. Most reporters have little time for thorough investigation. They depend on groups such as yours to do some of their research.

Using the condo conversion bill example again, let's say you want the press to do a story about the effects of condo conversion on the rental housing market in your city now and in the next decade. You are far more likely to sell this idea if you can show the reporter a study about those effects. If no one has done such a study, do some of the research yourself and present the results to a reporter in a press release. Then, the reporter needs only to call up some of your sources to verify the accuracy of your information.

On the Record/Off the Record.   When talking to reporters, always clarify which information can and cannot be attributed to you or your group. Unless you specify that something should be "off the record," and unless the reporter agrees, he or she may assume that everything said is "on the record." *Think before you speak.* After interviews people frequently complain, "But I didn't say that." Nine times out of ten they did, but they forgot—until they saw it in print and regretted it.

When it's necessary to state some information off the record, adhere to these precautions: *Before even beginning to relate the information, tell the reporter, "This must be strictly off the record," and get the reporter's assent.* Do this only with reporters you trust. Again, when resuming your comments for the record, say so.

It sounds easy, but it's also easy to forget because you will be so busy trying to be articulate, accurate, and all the rest. Until you are fairly comfortable at speaking to reporters, stay on the record; choose statements you will be satisfied with later.

Last but Not Least, Deadlines.   Deadlines are the name of the game in journalism. It's been said before, and will be said again: Find out the deadline for each news outlet and make sure you speak to reporters well before those times. Ask reporters how closely to deadline you can feed them information. This will depend partly on the kind of news medium it is. Print media may need the news further ahead of deadline than the electronic media do.

If you do not adhere to deadlines, your group and your issue will suffer because your side of the story may be omitted from the report that goes into print or on the air.

Communication Skills

The essence of all good publicity is effective communication. Below are some general rules on speaking and writing effectively, followed by some specific examples of communication tools used in lobbying campaigns.

Organization

Identify the Most Important Points. What must the audience know? An easy way to tackle this is to start with the "Five W" questions—Who, What, Where, When, and Why. This information often covers about fifty percent of what you have to say. Add to it the question, "How," and you've got another 10 to 15 percent. The rest will be details painting a clearer picture. These details can be examples, anecdotes, humor, drama, description, and quotes.

Arrange These Points in the Order of Importance. Put the most important point first, then the next most important, and so on. In longer statements, each point can introduce its own paragraph. In shorter statements, such as public service announcements and press releases, cram the answers to the Five W's into the first few sentences. Within these sentences, put the most important information first. If the most important point is the time and place of a meeting, put that first. If the most important point is the purpose of the meeting (or its topic, or famous speaker, or its size), put those items first.

Use a Paragraph as the Basic Unit for Each Point. In longer pieces, develop each point into a paragraph. State the basic point clearly in the first sentence of the paragraph. Follow it with information or examples illustrating the point or describing it in more detail.

Use a "Hook" to Get the Audience to Read or to Listen. A hook is a gripping anecdote or an interesting quotation to nab the reader's interest. For longer pieces, start with a one-paragraph anecdote, followed by the important information. Then, show how the anecdote relates to your basic points.

Let's say you are writing a press release for the local papers about an upcoming tenants' meeting at which your local senator will speak about the condo conversion bill. Though this piece will be called a press release, write it well enough that the local paper could use it as a news story with very little rewriting. For example:

> *Mary Campbell, an 81-year-old grandmother of three, used to live in a two-room apartment on Green Street. But now she lives in the public library, under bus shelters, and on park benches. Why? Because Mary's building was turned into condominiums too expensive for her to buy. And, so far, Mary has been unable to find another apartment she can afford on her social security check.*
>
> *Mary is not alone. The number of people made homeless due to condo conversion is growing rapidly. This problem will be discussed by Senator Goodheart in a meeting of the Mass. Tenants' Association on February 23, 8 p.m., in the First Congregational Church, 621 Main Street, Plackville.*

Commonwealth
Coalition for Literacy
447 Boston Plaza, Suite 3200
Arlington, MA 02188

December 27, 1988
Contact: Maureen Houlihan
(617) 555-1306

PRESS ADVISORY

Advocates for Adult Literacy to March on Beacon Hill

Statewide groups representing teachers, adult learners and
volunteer literacy tutors from adult basic education and English
as a second language programs will visit their senators and
representatives at the State House on Tuesday, January 3,
followed by a 12:30 rally on the Boston Common in front of the
State House.

Patricia Brown, president of the Commonwealth Coalition for
Literacy, will be the featured speaker at the 12:30 rally and
will be joined by Senator Edward M. Kennedy and Commonwealth
Literacy Campaign director Gerry D'Amico.

- ### -

A press advisory.

*Senator Goodheart, an active proponent of the "condo conver-
sion" bill (S.389), says the bill will help people like Mary Campbell
by . . ."*

Hooks can introduce very short statements, too. A radio public
service announcement for the same meeting could go like this:

*Have you seen more elderly citizens sleeping on park benches late
at night? Have you looked for an apartment lately, only to find that
most of them are "going condo"?*

*Help stop condominium conversion in Plackville. Senator Good-
heart will tell you how at a meeting on Tuesday, February 23, at 8
p.m. at the First Congregational Church, 621 Main St. For more
information, call. . . .*

An even shorter version would be:

Sick and tired of condo conversion in Plackville? Sen. Goodheart will tell you how to stop it. Come to a meeting . . .

Tone and Idiom

The tone and idiom should suit the audience. Above all, speak to your audience in its own language. If you break all the other rules, adhere to this one. People respond best when you speak to them directly. Picture the people you are talking (or writing) to; speak or write as if you were communicating in person. In conversation, most people automatically alter their language to suit their listeners. We simplify our speech for children and clean it up when speaking to persons in authority. Do the same in publicity messages. Use fancy language only if your audience also uses it—and will like it. Avoid technical jargon about your bill unless you know the audience understands those terms.

Your language and tone should also match those used in the newspaper, magazine, or station where the message will appear. Don't place a deadly serious ad in the *National Lampoon* or in *Mad Magazine*. Use a cartoon, a joke, or a light style for these magazines. Conversely, use a serious tone for magazines or programs that treat the news soberly.

Style

A good writing or speaking style is one which states things clearly, forcefully, and concisely. The audience should understand the speaker or writer with little or no effort. There are some simple tricks to strengthen and clarify your prose. Each section below includes one of these tricks, followed by examples of its application. The less desirable form of expression will appear in the left-hand column; an improved version of the same thought appears at the right.

State Things Positively.   Whenever possible, use positive rather than negative statements. Avoid using the word "not" because it is vague. It explains only by omission. Instead, tell us what is; that's much clearer.

Negative	*Positive*
We don't want condo conversion.	We want to protect rental housing.
Don't forget to write to your representative and senator today.	Write to your representative and senator today.

Use the Active Voice.   Statements made in the active, rather than the passive, voice are more forceful. In the active voice, the subject does something; in the passive voice, the subject seems like an innocent bystander rather than a moving force. Usually the active voice is more concise, too.

Passive	*Active*
The condo conversion bill was received by W&M on Monday, the 21st. The condo-related evictions were mentioned in his opening remarks.	W&M received the condo conversion bill on Monday, the 21st. He spoke about the condo-related evictions in his opening remarks.

Eliminate Unnecessary Words.   After writing something, drop out all unnecessary words; strive for conciseness. Get to the point immediately. This doesn't mean that you have to omit important details or use only short sentences, but every word should be necessary to communicate your thought. Cut out the dead wood.

Flabby	*Concise*
We need the help of all of you to get this bill successfully passed as soon as possible. The meeting is scheduled to be held on Tuesday evening at 8 p.m.	We need everyone's help to pass this bill during this legislative session. The meeting will begin at 8 a.m. on Tuesday.

Use Specific, Concrete Language.   Specific, concrete details paint a picture with words. The more details you present, the more colorful the picture and the more clear the lines. Replace vague statements with specific ones.

Vague	*Specific*
We had a positive response from the senators. Everyone must work hard on the condo conversion bill.	The senators liked the bill, and six of them agreed to support it on the floor. Everyone must call or write his/her rep, requesting support for the condo conversion bill on the House floor next week.

Avoid Strings of Long, Loose Sentences.   They become hard to follow and monotonous in rhythm. Break them up with short, punchy statements.

Run-on	*Concise*
Six of us met Senator Goodheart on Tuesday to discuss the condo conversion bill, but the meeting was disappointing because the senator kept avoiding direct responses to our questions and wouldn't commit himself definitely to supporting the bill.	Six of us met Senator Goodheart on Tuesday to discuss the condo conversion bill. But we were disappointed with the senator's response. He avoided direct answers to our questions and evaded a firm commitment to support the bill.

The short statements stand out amid the longer ones; use them to emphasize certain details within the paragraph.

Put the Most Emphatic Words at the Ends of Sentences. Words at the ends of sentences get the most stress; that's where the most important ones belong. This gives your writing and speaking more force.

In Middle	*At End*
Condo conversion threatens the well-being of many low-income tenants in our city. We hope Ms. Smith will be elected the new president.	In our city, many low-income tenants live under the constant threat of condo conversion. We hope the new president will be Ms. Smith.

For more on these and other rules of style and usage, read *The Elements of Style,* by William Strunk, Jr., and E.B. White, an excellent 85-page book summarizing the most important points of good writing.

Communication Tools Used in Publicity Campaigns

Press Releases

A press release should be brief—a couple of paragraphs for announcements of meetings or developments on the bill, and no more than two pages for news on reports, studies, or events connected with the bill. Use the shorter kind for informing the State House press of events you want them to cover. Use the longer kind for local media; though these are called press releases, they are actually short articles which can be used almost verbatim by the news outlet. Local outlets usually have small staffs; so, well-written material from contributors is often used with little or no rewriting.

Here's a sample of a short press release:

> *A public hearing on the "stop condo conversion" bill will be held by the Urban Affairs Committee on Thursday, March 19, at 10 a.m., State House Room 319. The bill's sponsor, Senator Jack Goodheart, says, "We expect a large turnout for this hearing." For more information, contact Senator Goodheart's office, 727-0010, or Gerry Arnold, Mass. Tenants' Association, 838-9670.*

Be sure that press releases include the names and phone numbers of people to contact for more information and the connection of these people to the bill.

The longer release would include the same kind of information, but it might start with a hook. For example:

> *According to a study released by the Massachusetts Urban Planning Department, by 1990 one-third of all Massachusetts apartments will be owned instead of rented. "Rental apartments may be a thing*

"But the learning centers don't have a lot of cash and will not survive even a short delay in funding," added Brown.

Recent studies show that there are more than 600,000 adults in Massachusetts who cannot read above the fourth grade level and one in three adults lack a high school diploma.

- more -

Commonwealth
Coalition for Literacy

447 Boston Plaza, Suite 3200
Arlington, MA 02188

January 3, 1989
Contact: Maureen Houlihan
(617) 555-1306

FOR RELEASE P.M. TUESDAY

Advocates for Adult Literacy March on Beacon Hill

Hundreds of supporters from around the state gathered at the State House today to demand the release of state funds for adult literacy programs in Massachusetts.

"It is unconscionable that the legislature favors withholding funds already allocated to learning centers," said Patricia Brown, president of the Commonwealth Coalition for Literacy. "We must let our elected officials know their constituents are here in force and watching their every step," she warned.

The legislature is slated to vote on recommending the withholding of funds pending a major bureaucratic reorganization of literacy and employment training agencies.

"Simply put, the lawmakers are holding a gun to the head of the already impoverished adult learning centers until the state agencies can agree on a new consolidated system," said Brown.

- more -

A press release.

of the past if this trend continues at the present rate for another 30 years," says Alberta Dearthpot, author of the study.

The report also shows: (1) as the number of rental units decreases, the average rent will increase; (2) by 1990 two-bedroom apartments in urban areas will average $560/month without utilities; (3) one-bedroom apartments will be unaffordable to individuals earning less than $25,000/year; and (4) the number of one-person households living in apartments alone will decrease by 20 percent.

Ms. Dearthpot will discuss the report at a meeting of the Mass. Tenants' Association on Tuesday, Feb. 8, at 7:30 p.m. in the Plackville Public Library.

For more information about the report, call Ms. Dearthpot, 727-9080; for more information about the meeting, call Ira Spat, 441-6756.

Press Advisory

A press advisory notifying the State House press corps of an upcoming press conference is similar to the short press release shown above. Stress who is addressing the conference and on which topics. Put all this information in the first sentence, if possible. For example:

A new Department of Urban Planning study on the effects of condo conversion on rental housing in Massachusetts will be released at a press conference on Tuesday, March 19, at 10 a.m. in the State House, Room 317. Mrs. Alberta Dearthpot, author of the study, and Senator Jack Goodheart, sponsor of the "Stop Condo Conversion Bill" (S.389), will address the conference.

The new study could affect passage of the bill on the Senate floor next Thursday.

For more information, call Senator Goodheart's office, 727-0010, or Gerry Arnold, Mass. Tenants' Association, 838-9670.

Call to an Assignment Editor

To get television coverage of a press conference, call the assignment editor at each station. Following is a sample conversation with an assignment editor:

"Hello. My name is Ira Spat, and I'm a member of the Mass. Tenants' Association. Tomorrow there will be a press conference to release a new Department of Urban Planning study on the effects of condo conversion on the rental housing market in Massachusetts. Alberta Dearthpot, the author of the study, and Senator Jack Goodheart, the sponsor of the "Stop Condo Conversion Bill," will talk about the findings and how they could affect the passage of the

condo bill in the Senate next week. Also, an evicted tenant will be available for an interview in her apartment.

"The conference will be held at 10 a.m. in Room 317 of the State House. Do you think you could send over one of your reporters to cover it?

"Do you want any background information about the bill or the study before the conference? If the reporter wants some background material, he can contact me at . . ."

The Thirty Second Interview

When television and radio reporters cover important campaign events, they often splice together short reactions to those events by members of the different factions. If your bill clears a hurdle in the legislature, be prepared to give a short statement to the press. Decide what's the one most important point to get on the air—and be able to say it in one, or at most, two sentences.

Let's say the Stop Condo Bill has passed in the Senate and is now going to the House. A victory for your group. What should you say when they put a mike in front of you:

"I'd like to thank Senator Goodheart for his hard work in passing this bill." Or,

"The tenants of Massachusetts thank Senator Goodheart and everyone else who helped to get this bill passed in the Senate." Or,

"This a great victory for tenants' rights in Massachusetts."

The Public Service Announcement

The public service announcement (PSA) is a short announcement for radio or television about a meeting or event. Like the short press release, it must pack the answers to the Five W questions into a couple of sentences. It can begin with a short hook:

"Sick of condo conversion in your neighborhood? Come to a meeting of the Mass. Tenants' Association to find out how you can help pass the new Stop Condo law. The meeting is on Wednesday, March 1st, at 7:30 p.m. at the Plackville Public Library. Call 838-9670 for more information."

These announcements should be written exactly as you want them read on the air. Call stations well in advance of your event to find out when the PSA's must be submitted in order to be aired. Each station has different rules about this. Many of them want PSA's to be submitted two or three weeks in advance. Sometimes this is impossible in a fast-paced lobbying campaign, but try to meet their deadlines whenever possible.

Chapter 9

IMPLEMENTATION BLUES

Congratulations!! You got your bill passed into law! You had to jump through all the required hoops of the legislative process for two consecutive years; you had to compromise a little bit along the way. But you did it! With the help of a motivated, organized network of affected constituents, a team of responsive, committed legislative sponsors and a sympathetic Governor, a new law will go into the law books requiring your state government to do something about the problem that got you and your network started in the first place.

"Now," says a weary coordinating committee, happy to be through with the frustrating task of talking elected officials into what they should have been doing in the first place, "lets hope they do it right."

"Oh, dear," says the lobbyist under her breath, happy to be through talking the coordinating committee into doing what they should have been doing in the first place, "I hope I'm not going to spending the rest of my life making sure they do."

It usually is the lobbyist who first gets the sinking feeling that the lobbying campaign will never end, and that the passing of a bill is only the first step. A good lobbyist has learned the hard way that all institutions have to be prodded and poked to move in a different direction. The legislature had to be prodded and poked to pass the bill. The organization that filed the bill and engaged the services of the lobbyist had to be prodded and poked into building an effective network. The bureaucracies of the administration will have to be prodded and poked to implement the new law.

To implement a law means that the administration must start doing something new to meet the requirements of the new law. If your bill created a new program, the administration may have to

Congratulations! You got your bill passed into law.

hire new people, find and equip an office, create new application forms, and write new regulations. If your bill stopped an existing practice, they may have to fire or transfer staff, redesign existing forms, or write new regulations.

A new law may be implemented in a month, a year, or never at all. The state may implement a new law exactly the way the authors intended, or they may not.

Welcome to the "Implementation Blues!"

This chapter will discuss the most usual causes for delay in the implementation of a new program and suggest specific strategies to speed things up. In any implementation process there is a given sequence of activities that must happen, such as people to hire and regulations to write. For every activity there is a person in charge of making decisions that produce an outcome, such as a national search for a new director or the appointment of a political hack. *An implementation campaign is a set of strategies and tactics to influence the outcome of the bureaucratic decision making.*

Your job is to get the new program started up and to make sure they do it right. Both jobs utilize the two rules of lobbying: (1) Elected and appointed decision makers make different decisions when watched by the affected constituency; and (2) lobbying is just getting the right information to the right person at the right time.

Before You Begin

Figure out how soon your bill will become law. It will be different in every state, but all states have some sort of a "waiting period" before a bill becomes effective. In Massachusetts, the constitution clearly outlines the rules.

Ninety-Day Bills

Most legislation takes effect ninety days after it has become law. More specifically, it becomes law ninety days after:

- the Governor has signed it; or
- the legislature has overridden the Governor's veto; or
- ten days (not counting Sundays and holidays) have expired from the time the Governor receives a bill on which he has taken no action.

In addition, the legislature can require that a law take effect later than the ninety-day period by simply writing a later date into it. The legislature, however, cannot shorten the ninety-day period, except in the situations discussed below.

Emergency Measures

In general, emergency measures take effect on the date of approval. Only the legislature or the Governor can declare that a law is an emergency measure. This is how it's done.

By the Legislature. The legislature can place an emergency preamble on a bill by passing a motion to this effect with a 2/3 standing vote in each branch on the preamble only. This vote is taken first in the House and then in the Senate, and it always comes before the vote for enactment. (At this time, a roll call vote can be requested by only two senators or five representatives instead of the normal 1/5 of the senators present or 20 representatives.) If the bill is passed with an emergency preamble attached, it goes first to the House and then to the Senate for final enactment.

If either branch fails to adopt the emergency preamble, the bill is returned to the legislature engrossing division to be re-engrossed without the preamble. In this case, it is sent to the House and Senate for final enactment without the preamble. The bill then takes effect in the usual ninety-day period unless it has been given a later effective date or it's passed as a thirty-day bill. (See section below for more on thirty-day bills.)

By the Governor.   Although the legislature has to go through all the above steps to attach an emergency preamble on a bill, the Governor can simply do so when he signs it. He can do this even if the legislature has already rejected an emergency preamble. It does not have to be approved by anyone else.

Thirty-Day Bills

Certain bills take effect thirty days after enactment. These bills deal with: (1) the powers, creation, or abolition of courts; (2) the appointment, qualifications, tenure, removal, or compensation of judges; (3) subjects restricted to a particular town; (4) appropriations of money for the current or ordinary expenses of the Commonwealth; and (5) religion.

Mixed Subjects

Occasionally, a bill passes containing some provisions which would fall into the thirty-day category and others which would fall into the typical ninety-day rule. Common practice deals with these bills as a whole and treats them as ninety-day, not thirty-day, laws. But this is still an open question. Some believe these bills should be either thirty-day or ninety-day; others favor allowing the separate provisions to carry different effective dates. Very few bills fall into this confusing category—thank goodness!

Assessing the Need for Action

Identify the Agency and the Person Responsible.   Somewhere in one of the state office buildings sit the persons assigned to implement your law. Your job is to find them. If you specified the administrative agency in your bill, start your search with the head of the agency. If your bill was vague about the administrative agency, make a note never to do *that* again, and start at the Governor's office and work down through the Secretaries, the Commissioners, the Directors and all of their assistants until you find the persons in charge.

Determine the Need for New Regulations. Before a new program or process can begin, the administering state agency may have to issue official regulations. Regulations take the theory of the law and make it into practice by specifying procedures and processes not included in the law itself, such as application deadlines and staff qualifications. For instance, a law permitting public housing residents to keep pets might be accompanied by regulations that not only specify the number, size, and species of approved pets but forbid the keeping of goats and alligators.

Regulations have the force of law, and the process for issuing regulations is laid out very specifically in state statutes. (Accompanied of course by more regulations on how to issue regulations.) This "rule-making process" allows for public access and input, including public hearings and solicitation of public comment on draft regulations.

You may have included in your bill a requirement that the administering agency issue regulations. You may discover that even your simple little three-line bill stopping the state from doing something will require new regulations. In either case, there is an existing process for issuing regulations in your state with a rigid timetable and procedures. The Secretary of State's office is the place to go to find out the procedure in your state.

Administrative Cost—the Budget. If your bill set up a whole new program requiring the state to hire new people, rent space, install telephones, and buy office supplies, they will either use existing staff, space, telephones, and office supplies or they will have to hire, rent, install, and buy some more. If your bill did not include an appropriation, and if the state is not willing or able to use existing staff and office space for your law, you must run a budget campaign to get the legislature to appropriate the money needed to implement your law. Yes, back to the legislative arena for another campaign.

Organizational Resources. Determine your organization's ability and willingness to follow through on an implementation campaign. Turn back to Chapter 1 in this book and ask yourself the same questions you asked before you started your lobbying campaign. While an implementation campaign does not incur the printing and postage costs involved in a lobbying campaign, it takes a comparable amount of time to participate in all the necessary meetings.

Do you have a campaign committee, and an organized network ready to push and prod the administration? In an implementation campaign, the committee members and the lobbyist will participate in negotiations with the administration. While there is less for a network to do in an implementation campaign, it is important to keep them informed and up to date. They provide the power base for the committee and the lobbyist by just "being there." The committee members will be participating in negotiation sessions with the administration and reporting back to the network. The committee will meet at least monthly. Plan on four updates a year to your network.

Do you have the money to pay a part-time lobbyist or a volunteer to staff the campaign? The lobbyist should plan on spending two days a week in meetings (or trying to get one) at the state office buildings.

Do you have the money to pay an attorney or have a volunteer to work with you on the rule-making process? While regulations are easier to read and understand than the law they complement, it's important to find a professional to be your advocate in the beginning of the process.

Assess any opposition. Opposition to an implementation campaign may come from individuals or agencies inside the administration, or it may come from old adversaries from the legislature. Your lobbying campaign should have surfaced almost everyone, but sometimes opponents appear even at this late date. You can be sure of one thing: Your old opposition didn't go away. You may have compromised with them, you may have out-lobbied them, you may have humiliated them. But they didn't go away.

Try to find out if they are going to try to delay the implementation process, or try to bring up their old issues during the regulatory process, or try to stop your budget campaign. If they opposed you during the lobbying campaign, you have some sense of their strength, and determination. Even if they didn't oppose you very vigorously, you must assume that an opponent with an established relationship with the administrative agency will try to slow down or stop the implementation process.

You cannot dismiss any opponents lightly. While the legislative process is public, with hundred of players and plenty of witnesses, an implementation process is a relatively private affair, with lots of opportunities for reasonable-sounding delays and compromises.

Assess your allies. The original legislative sponsors and supporters of your bill should be on the top of your outside allies list. Nothing makes legislators madder than the administration not implementing a new program or process they worked so hard to create. Pull out the list from your lobbying campaign and prioritize individuals and agencies who may have longstanding relationships with your administering agency. You will find it easier to involve timid outside allies now that you have a record of winning.

The list of inside allies starts with the Governor and the members of his staff who advised him to sign your bill. (You can force your inside opposition to back off, or at least sneak around by keeping the Governor informed about the inside opposition within his own administration.)

Other inside allies will be attracted to the public visibility and credibility your campaign will bring state government. Most managers go through their entire public service careers in total anonymity, making decisions every day costing millions of dollars and affecting thousands of people. If you and your organization use the two rules of lobbying, those decision makers will be better informed by affected constituents who appreciate an enlightened manager's hard work and know how to say thank you.

Is implementation a public or nonpublic issue? All implementation campaigns start out nonpublic. Even if your lobbying campaign was a very public issue on the front page of the papers for six months, you are now in a very nonpublic phase of implementation. The press and the public think the campaign is over. You won. Enjoy it as long as you can and keep a low profile until you figure out the kind of cooperation you'll get from the administration.

You can always go public, if you decide you must, when you can point to specific, deliberate action by the administration that either advances or delays the implementation process. For instance, getting good press when something wonderful happens, such as the appointment of an advisory board, or the hiring of the first director will reinforce a positive relationship with the administrative agency. Putting together a press conference of legislative sponsors denouncing the new draft regulations will force the administrative agency to choose between making enemies in the legislature or rewriting the regulations. Direct action techniques such as office sit-ins and picket lines are good for getting your organization's rank and file participating in a powerful tactic and for providing a story for the press to cover. (For more on the press, read Chapter 8.)

Mounting an Implementation Campaign

Example One

You've identified the agency responsible for administering your new program, which provides information and referral services for hard-to-place adoptable children. Your bill was accompanied by an adequate six-month budget. The Commissioner met with you and the steering committee, and introduced you to the Assistant Deputy for Planning who is "the person" in charge of start-up. The Assistant Deputy for Planning has the following timetable for implementation.

- *Within 60 days:* finding temporary borrowed space and recruiting and hiring a director, administrative assistant, and secretary.
- *Within 120 days:* drafting temporary regulations, projecting a full year's budget, appointing an advisory board, and beginning delivery of limited services.
- *Within 180 days:* moving into independent space, issuing final regulations, and achieving full program implementation.

You ask how you can help. The Commissioner encourages you to work closely with the Assistant Deputy to write the job description for the Director and to help him screen the candidates for the Director. He asks you for nominations from your organization for the advisory board, promises that you will have complete access to the drafting of the regulations, and closes by asking if you all will be able to meet with him and the Assistant Deputy once a month for updates and reports.

What do you do? You agree to work with the Assistant Deputy on all the items outlined above, and you thank them for the meeting. The implementation campaign for your organization will form subcommittees to follow up on each item with the Commissioner.

Example Two

Two years ago you filed a bill to set up a new agency to coordinate information and referral services for hard-to-place adoptable children. The Governor opposed your bill because he viewed it as an unnecessary layer of bureaucracy, pointing to an existing agency that could administer such a program. You compromised to get his support and redrafted your bill to give the Department of Social Services the authority to administer the program. You tried to get the Department's budget increased in a budget campaign but failed, partly because the Commissioner told Ways and Means he could carry out the mandates of the law with existing staff.

Two months after the Governor signed your bill, you get a meeting with the Commissioner. He brings in the person responsible for the program, who is merely compiling and circulating a list of all the hard-to-place adoptable children. While they seem sincere, it is clear to you and your delegation that your bill is not being fully implemented.

What do you do next? During the meeting you gather as much information as you can about the specific activities being carried out by the agency. The implementation campaign for your organization includes the formation of a subcommittee to document the lack of implementation and plan a strategy to hold the administration accountable, starting with the Commissioner and ending with the Governor.

Example Three

After almost two years of angry meetings, indignant press conferences, and threats to sue, it is clear that the administration has no intention of implementing an information and referral service for hard-to-place adoptable children. Your legislative sponsors are on to other crusades, the press is bored with your story, and your organization is disheartened and discouraged.

What do you do next? Decide if you can manage to raise the stakes higher. Do you have a winnable case, the budget to pay a lawyer, and the two years to wait for the courts to decide? Can you mount a hard-hitting direct action campaign with sit-ins and picket lines targeted at embarrassing the administration into responding? Both tactics will bar any further negotiations, but negotiating hasn't gotten you very far.

The Elements of an Implementation Campaign

Few new laws are implemented as quickly and with so much co-operation as the case laid out in Example One. The tasks are laid out clearly, the timetable is realistic, and the end is in sight.

Only rarely does an administration under siege continue flatly to refuse to implement a new law like the case laid out in Example Three. It is very difficult for a volunteer membership organization to last more than a few years in such a campaign without resorting to the courts or the streets.

The most likely situation would be a variation of Example Two, with a well-meaning overburdened bureaucrat making do with too little staff.

The tone and the attitude of your implementation campaign is important. The "target" of your lobbying campaign was the institution of state government, and your goal was to impose change through the institution of the legislature. The target of an implementation campaign is likely to be one or two people in the middle of the bureaucracy, and your goal is to impose change on them. Your campaign will be much more up close and personal, and your attitude and approach should be solicitous and supportive. Consider them your allies until they prove otherwise.

A smart bureaucrat tries hard to find allies who can provide credibility for the agency with the press and fight the external and internal battles for resources by lobbying the Governor and legislature for more money. You can negotiate from a position of power because your group is ready to provide that political support for a program they care very much about.

The Securing of an Adequate Budget. If they tell you they can't get your new program started immediately because there isn't enough money, ask them how much is enough. Ask them for the budget breakdown while you're at it. Budgets are public documents. Budgets are broken down into categories, sometimes called subsidiary accounts such as personnel, supplies, travel, and so forth. There will be a person in the agency budget department who has broken down the budget at least three times. The first version is the ideal budget, if they had all the money they needed. The second version is what they could live with, and the third is probably what they got.

What do you do with all these back-up budgets? You offer to help by supporting the Commissioner's requests for more money. It is perfectly appropriate for affected constituents to lobby the administration and the legislature to adequately fund a state program. Simply move forward using the two rules of lobbying. Go up the ladder in the administration, and call on your allies in the legislature. You have a reasonable chance of finding someone in the administration or in the legislature who can identify a hidden pot of reserve funds somewhere and wave a magic wand to transfer funds through some back door account to bail out your program.

Sometimes a Commissioner will tell you that he cannot appeal "upstairs" or in the legislature without jeopardizing his job. He may be telling the truth, or he may be saving his chances to appeal for a more favored program; it doesn't matter. You can and should move without him. They can't fire you.

Getting a Good Director and Advisory Board. These appointments raise important considerations for an organized affected constituency: Are they going to try to coopt us and defuse us by hiring one of us and putting the rest of us on the advisory board?

Probably.

Who knows the problem and the solution better, after all. Who has established credibility in the legislature, in the press, through-

Cutting through all the red tape.

out the advocacy world. (Who has been muttering for two years, "I can't believe I used to be intimidated by these people. Why, I've got more ability in my little finger. . . .")

You will definitely be asked to nominate members of your organization for any advisory board. There may be a person on your lobbying campaign committee with all the necessary credentials for the Director's job. Think through and discuss the impact of such appointments on your organization and on the implementation campaign. Here are some questions to consider.

Do you have an organizational replacement for the person being considered? One cannot serve two masters, and a person certainly cannot be involved in an implementation campaign from the outside while at the same time publicly accountable on the inside as a staff or advisory board member. Organization members appointed to staff or advisory board positions will have to keep a professional distance from the campaign.

Can you do more good inside? Sometimes talented newcomers in a supportive administration can move mountains of red tape and be tremendously effective—especially if their work is generally endorsed by their old affected constituency organization.

What happens when we have to disagree? Trouble comes when old friends have to get professional and can't (or won't) deliver on a promised timetable, or can't (or won't) change a bad policy. Suddenly an ally is transformed into opposition and a target of the implementation campaign to boot. You can try to prepare potential appointees for the inevitable charges of betrayal and sell-out, but it will hurt anyway.

Whether or not anyone from your organization is recruited for any position, you may be asked to suggest names or to sit on a "screening committee" to interview candidates. Both activities are very helpful in building a good relationship with the administration. If someone in your organization is in the human resources field and is willing to spend hours reviewing resumes and doing interviews, this is a good subcommittee assignment. Otherwise common sense prevails.

Writing Good Regulations.   It's helpful to have an attorney familiar with the rule-making process involved during the drafting and publishing of the regulations, if only to provide protection from intimidating bureaucrats speaking legalese. The key to getting good regulations is getting informal, unofficial access at the drafting and redrafting stage.

Smart administrators welcome input at the drafting stage and encourage the legal department to work closely with affected constituencies. They know that they have nothing to lose and much to gain in good will and information. Not-so-smart administrators have to be coaxed and coddled and convinced that your input in the drafting stage won't let the fox in the chicken coop.

After the draft regulations are written, they are officially published and hearings are scheduled to get official public input. Oral

The Commonwealth of Massachusetts
SECRETARY OF STATE

REGULATION FILING AND PUBLICATION

1. REGULATION CHAPTER NUMBER AND HEADING:

211 CMR 40.00 -69.00   HEALTH INSURANCE

2. NAME OF AGENCY:

DIVISION OF INSURANCE

3. THIS DOCUMENT IS REPRINTED FROM THE CODE OF MASSACHUSETTS REGULATIONS AND CONTAINS THE FOLLOWING:

211 CMR 40.00 MARKETING OF HEALTH INSURANCE
41.00 ADVERTISEMENTS OF ACCIDENT AND SICKNESS INSURANCE
42.00 MINIMUM STANDARDS OF FULL AND FAIR DISCLOSURE FOR THE FORM AND CONTENTS OF ACCIDENT AND SICKNESS INSURANCE SOLD IN THE COMMONWEALTH OF MASSACHUSETTS
43.00 HEALTH MAINTENANCE ORGANIZATIONS
44.00 OPINION, FINDINGS AND ORDER RELATIVE TO A FILING OF A MASSACHUSETTS BLUE CROSS, INC. FOR A NON-GROUP BLUE CROSS RATES PROPOSED TO BE EFFECTIVE ON BILLINGS DATES AS THEY OCCUR COMMENCING MAY 1, 1972
45.00 ESTABLISHMENT OF SERVICE FEE TO AGENTS AND BROKERS ASSISTING EMPLOYERS IN OBTAINING WORMEN'S COMPEMSATION INSURANCE
46.00 OPINIONS, FINDINGS, AND DECISIONS ON 1975 WORKMEN'S COMPENSATION RATES RENDERED MAY, 1975

ACCIDENT AND SICKNESS INSURANCE

be deeme...
...

without a clear and conspicuous disclosure of the following:
(a) The extent and nature of the coverage offered.
(b) The extent to which the coverage meets the potential risk.
(c) The cost of the coverage.
It is therefore the intent of 211 CMR 40.00 to identify as misrepresentative any trade practice which solicits an offer to contract for health insurance without disclosing the above data.

40.02: Applicability

(1) 211 CMR 40.00 shall apply to any health insurance marketing method, as that term is hereinafter defined, intended for presentation, distribution or dissemination in Massachusetts when such presentation, distribution or dissemination is made either directly or indirectly by or on behalf of any person as defined herein.

(2) Every insurer as herein defined shall establish and at all times maintain a system of control over the content, form and method of dissemination of all marketing methods of its policies. All such marketing methods regardless of by whom written, created, designed or presented, shall be the responsibility of the insurer whose policies are so marketed.

40.03: Definitions

(1) A marketing method for the purpose of 211 CMR 40.00 shall include any of the following when they are used by any person with the intent of soliciting an offer to contract for health insurance:
(a) Printed and published material, audio-visual material and descriptive literature used in direct mail. newspapers, magazines, radio scripts, TV scripts, billboards and similar displays; and
(b) Descriptive literature and sales aids of all kinds issued for presentation to members of the insurance buying public, including but not limited to circulars, leaflets, booklets, depictions, illustrations and form letters; and

12/31/86

Final regulations.

and written testimony is taken from the public at this time, and anyone can suggest changes in regulations. Final regulations are then published, ideally taking into account the suggestions offered during the hearings. This official part of the process is sometimes called the promulgation of regulations, and if you can't get informal access, you certainly should offer testimony at the hearing. Your opposition certainly will.

If the final regulations are bad, you should have your attorney figure out if you can take some legal steps to re-open the regulation process again. If the final regulations are legal but inadequate, you will have to document the problems over time, hoping to build a case strong enough to pressure the administration to change them. You can also file a bill mandating the adoption of the regulations.

Odds and Ends.   Since anyone looking for trouble or work will usually find both, you and your organization will find yourselves tempted to get involved in some of the small administrative decisions such as hiring the receptionist or drafting the application form. Examine your resources and your motivations before volunteering your time or opinion. Resist exercising power for its own sake, but still be watchful for small decisions in the making that may send a very bad signal to the public. For instance, you might insist that the receptionist be bilingual or that the office be handicapped accessible.

Critical to your ability to see a big problem hiding in a small decision is a good informal relationship with your program's managers. Regular meetings to review the implementation process will flag most potential trouble and allow for internal correction.

Ongoing Monitoring and Support

OK. Your program is up and running. It started six months late, the Director is a little frazzled because the position for the administrative assistant got lost in the bowels of the budget bureau along with the authorization for the duplicating machine. Still, the program is up and running.

Now what?

You and your organization must decide if you are going to perform a monitoring function, providing ongoing analysis that will help to improve and upgrade the program, or whether you are going to continue a supporting function for the agency administrators.

The Monitoring Function.   To be credible, a monitoring effort requires technical analysis of the operation of the program based on thorough research done by recognized experts in the field. You will

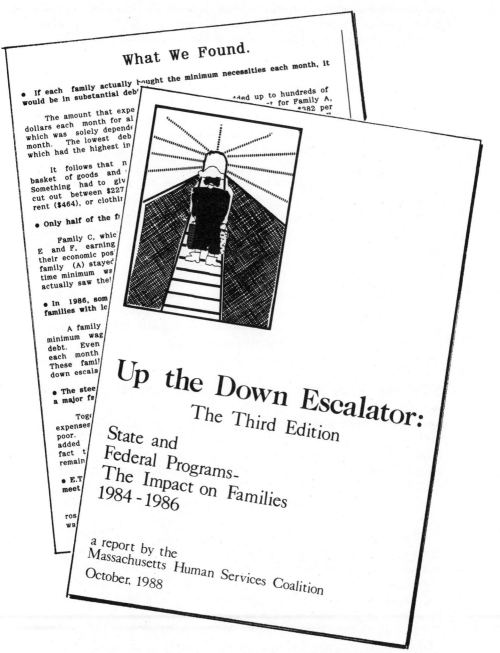

What We Found.

• If each family actually bought the minimum necessities each month, it would be in substantial deb'

The amount that expe dollars each month for al which was solely depende month. The lowest deb which had the highest in

It follows that n basket of goods and Something had to giv cut out between $227 rent ($464), or clothi

• Only half of the f

Family C, whic E and F, earning their economic pos' family (A) stayed time minimum wa actually saw the'

• In 1986, som families with lo

A family minimum wag debt. Even each month These famil down escala

• The stee a major fa

Tog expenses poor. added fact t remain

• E.T meet

ros wa

...ded up to hundreds of ...t for Family A, ...382 per

Up the Down Escalator:
The Third Edition

State and
Federal Programs-
The Impact on Families
1984 - 1986

a report by the
Massachusetts Human Services Coalition
October, 1988

A monitoring report published by the Massachusetts Human Services Coalition.

find yourself flying in expert witnesses from all over the country, printing 50-page statistical reports, and coordinating teams of attorneys to research a class action suit. The monitoring function is best carried out by a well-funded, established organization staffed by professionals.

Clearly, the monitoring function is *not* a campaign. Campaigns end when you win or lose; a monitoring function goes on forever—a sort of life sentence with no hope of parole. Finally, since the monitoring function is primarily in the hands of highly skilled professionals, there is little room for citizen advocates. And truthfully, after the sharp highs and lows of lobbying and implementation campaigns, many citizen advocates find the monitoring function boring.

Now after that pail of cold water, let me point out that many of the permanent well-funded organizations with professional staffs and public credibility started out as citizen advocacy groups lobbying and then helping to implement a new law. A particularly inspiring example here in Massachusetts is the parent group that lobbied through a first-in-the-nation law mandating special education programs for handicapped children. The parents eventually incorporated themselves into a nonprofit organization that raised money to hire a professional staff to carry out a very tough monitoring and enforcement campaign in every city and town in the Commonwealth.

The Supporting Function.   The supporting function consists of trouble shooting at the request of the director or the advisory board. You may find yourselves testifying at Ways and Means to support an increased budget, or meeting with the Governor to request that he fill vacancies on the advisory board. You may find yourself at press conferences opening new offices or hosting state-wide training sessions for new staff.

Organizational Considerations.   While the supporting function is another life sentence, the tasks can be easily managed by a volunteer organization. Because you're always popping into one crisis after another, it's not boring. The biggest problem is organizational and personal burn-out. Some of your best and most experienced volunteers have moved away or out of the organization. It's past time for new leadership, and there is no better time to break them in than during the support phase.

You will still need a decision-making committee and a designated lobbyist to keep in formal contact with your program's director and advisory board. That formal contact can take the form of updates and policy reviews through the mail, accompanied by monthly meetings with the program managers. These same managers should "staff out" your organization for any public support activities, such as press conferences or legislative testimony, arranging everything from reserving rooms to typing up the press release.

The goal of the supportive function is to help your director expand and improve the program. Your activities will build a base of outside allies in the legislature and in the public. Since both parties have a direct self-interest in making the program better, it is important to cultivate an open and honest relationship between your organization and the director in order to reach that goal.

*   *   *

A final verse in implementation blues: This chapter is dedicated to those tenacious, patient, persistent citizen advocates who have laboriously plowed through ten different drafts of regulations, sat through dozens of interviews with aspiring bureaucrats, taken copious notes at endless briefing meetings, and summarized it all in an easy-to-read memo. They exert a tremendous influence over the administration of state government and command enormous respect inside and outside the professional advocacy community. They don't think they're serving a life sentence. They don't think the monitoring or supporting function is boring. They're having fun.

APPENDICES

REGISTERING AS A MASSACHUSETTS LOBBYIST

by Ernest Winsor

In Massachusetts, when you start working as a lobbyist, or at the beginning of each calendar year, you should register as a lobbyist with the Secretary of State's office. This should be done within ten days of the earlier date. Massachusetts law defines a lobbyist, or **legislative agent,** as:

> . . . *any person who for compensation . . . does any act to . . . influence legislation . . . or to influence the decision of any member of the Executive branch [concerning legislation] . . . or the adoption, defeat, or postponement of a . . . rule or regulation. . . . The term shall include persons who, as part of their regular and usual employment and not simply incidental thereto, attempt to . . . influence legislation . . . whether or not any compensation in addition to the salary . . . is received for such services.*

This means that any person *whose employment includes lobbying—*legislative or administrative—should register. Persons who do not lobby regularly are not required to register, nor are volunteers, even if they lobby regularly and even if they are reimbursed for expenses such as traveling. But if you lobby regularly *and* are paid for it, you must register.

In addition to registering as a lobbyist, your employer must authorize your employment as your group's lobbyist. Although the law specifies slightly different times for filing these two forms, it's more efficient to file both at once. Accordingly, before leaving to register, you should take with you all of the following to avoid a hassle when you get there:

- *Authorization for Legislative Agent form* signed by your organization's chief executive offer, containing a blurb in the blank just above his or her signature describing the "Following Named Matter" in which you will act as legislative agent for your employer.

177

- *Three current photographs of yourself,* two 2 1/2 × 2 1/2 inches, the third 1 1/4 × 1 1/4 inches. Print your name on the back of each. Instant camera shots are probably the cheapest, and surely the quickest.
- *A check for $35.00* (the Secretary of State abhors cash) payable to the Commonwealth of Massachusetts.

With these materials assembled, go to the McCormack State Office Building, 1 Ashburton Place, Boston, Massachusetts. Deliver it anytime between 8:45 a.m. and 5:00 p.m.

In registering you will be asked to fill out a form printed on prenumbered pages of a ledger book. Most of the blanks on the form ask for obvious answers, but four of them might give you some trouble; these are explained below.

Mail Address.   Where the form calls for "Mail Address (if different)," put your work address if you want your lobbying credential and your periodic reporting forms sent to your office instead of to your home.

Date of Employment.   Where the form calls for "Date of Employment," enter the very date of your registration—unless you were hired at your job within the current year. In the latter case, enter the date you were hired.

Employer's Business Interests.   Where the form calls for "Employer's Business Interests Affected by Legislation," put the same blurb that was written on your employer's authorization form in the blank for "Following Named Matters." This describes the kinds of interests and matters on which you intend to lobby. Be sure to include *all* the possible areas you may have to cover, so that you aren't caught later being unauthorized to lobby a bill falling outside of your official range of interests.

By way of example, the following was the blurb Massachusetts Law Reform Institute (a legal services backup center) used for a staff attorney:

> . . . *representing the interests of low-income persons, defined as having net annual income at or below 125% of the federal poverty level on all matters before the Massachusetts Legislature.*

If your blurb is long and would be hard to read if handwritten, bring a typed copy on plain white paper, which will be pasted onto the ledger sheet by one of the Secretary of State's personnel.

In a month or so, you will receive a neat, little laminated ID card showing your name, your mug shot (the smaller picture), and some words describing you as a *legislative* lobbyist.

Congratulations! You are now a duly registered lobbyist.

POTENTIAL RESTRICTIONS ON LOBBYING

by Allan G. Rodgers

You are working for, or on behalf of, a nonprofit organization, and someone says, "You can't lobby. You'll lose your tax exemption." Or, "The foundation that funds us says we can't do that." Or, "The government agency that funds us has some severe restrictions on lobbying."

Not so! Every nonprofit group can do at least *some* lobbying and still receive or retain a federal tax exemption, foundation grants, and most federal funds. Let's look more closely at the rules.

Tax Exemption

A nonprofit organization can engage in an *insubstantial* amount of lobbying and still have federal tax exemption. A good rule of thumb is: You can devote at least *five percent* of your time and/or budget to lobbying activities, unless you *elect* to do more and then agree to keep meticulous records. (See below.) For this purpose, lobbying activities are defined as: (1) direct contacts with legislators by your employees or members (acting as such); or (2) appeals to others to make direct contacts with legislators. *Not* included are activities such as furnishing information, drafting legislation, training others to lobby, and doing research.

Under the Internal Revenue Code, you can file an **election** with the Internal Revenue Service and devote up to *20 percent* of your group's time to lobbying without endangering your tax-exempt status. But to qualify for this election, you must keep detailed records of your time and expenditures spent on lobbying activities.

Furthermore, federal tax laws allow foundations to give you money as long as you stay within the legal limits on lobbying activity. But some foundations prohibit their own grant monies from

179

being used for lobbying. Again, you can lobby, but you must use other funds—or you can distribute information or do other work on legislative issues that is not defined technically as lobbying. You should, therefore, keep good records of your spending to be sure no foundation money goes into lobbying.

If you're in doubt about the effects of lobbying on your organization's tax status, be sure to ask a lawyer or other tax adviser to examine your group's particular situation. Sometimes nonprofit organizations can get this kind of advice free of charge.

Government Funding Restrictions

Some government funding carries restrictions on lobbying. If your group receives such funds, first look carefully at the language of the restrictions. Most limitations prohibit certain ways of going about lobbying, rather than banning lobbying altogether. Most allow you to respond to requests to legislators for information and to lobby for your own agency's government funding. Some ban only lobbying through the media or similar public campaigns. Find out what you *can* do, and then adjust your legislative activities accordingly.

Registering as a Legislative Agent (Lobbyist)

Massachusetts state law requires anyone who is a **legislative agent** to register with the Secretary of State's office at the beginning of each year (or within ten days after starting legislative or state agency rulemaking activity). If you're an employee of a nonprofit organization, you have to register only if lobbying at the state level is a significant part of your job. But if you do *any* lobbying on state agency regulations, no matter how little, you have to register.

The annual fee for registration is $35, and you must file a report every six months. If you have any doubt about whether a particular individual should register, it's probably a good idea to do so.

To Sum Up

So, if you're in a nonprofit organization, you can lobby, but be sure to know which rules govern your group's legislative activities. Get good advice and keep careful records so you can show that you're following the law.

INFORMATION TREASURE TROVES AT THE MASSACHUSETTS STATE HOUSE

The House and Senate Clerks' Offices

If there is ever an award presented to the most cheerful, patient, accommodating staff in the Massachusetts State House, surely there would be a tie for it between the House and Senate Clerks' offices. Both sets of staff people consistently answer all questions by the misinformed and the unenlightened—even if those questions sound dumb. Ask them anything; if they don't know the answer, they'll tell you where to find it.

In addition to helpful personnel, the Clerks' offices also have printed information about legislation and legislative proceedings. The draft journals of the House and Senate's previous day's session are available there for reading on the premises. Advance calendars are available as well. Huge "Docket Books" list all the bills as they are filed but *before* they get an official number and go to the printer. So there is often a line of lobbyists waiting to get advance notice about bills that might affect their particular interests.

Each Clerk's office has a fulltime staff person sitting at the computer ready to answer any question regarding the status of any bill. They are just as polite over the phone as in person, so feel free to call them when you can't come in.

Both Clerks' offices are open weekdays from 8:00 a.m. to 5:00 p.m., also at any other times when the legislature is in session.

Document Room

The Document Room is open 9:00 a.m. to 5:00 p.m. during the week and weekends, and evenings, whenever the legislature is in session. The *House* and *Senate Calendars* for that day's session are usually available around 10:00 a.m. on days the legislature is in session. *Advance calendars* are available around 4:00 p.m. the working day *before* the session. The *Daily List* of committee hearings is usually available at 3:00 p.m. the day before the hearings. Advance notice of committee hearings can be obtained from *The Legislative Bulletin,* which is issued periodically (but irregularly) starting in February. Copies of all bills filed in December and late-filed during the session are available when they come back from the printer.

The printer does not catch up with the 8,000 bills filed in December until the following March. From that point on, you can count on a three- to five-day wait for a new or amended bill to appear in the Document Room—*after* it leaves the Clerks' offices.

When you want copies of or information about various bills, list them by branch and bill number—that is, if you want to stay on good terms with the people in the Document Room. Your list might look like this: H.12, H.376, H.4506; S.523, S.623, S.624.

Copies of all versions of the budget are also available in the Document Room, but always in short supply. If you want one, get there as soon as possible after the budget report leaves the Governor's office or a Ways and Means Committee.

Finally, the *House* and *Senate Journals* of each daily session are available, usually a month after that day's session. Drafts of these journals can be read in the House and Senate Clerks' offices the day following a session.

The State Library of Massachusetts

The library is open 8:45 a.m. to 5:00 p.m., five days a week. Very helpful staff are available to direct you to legislative documents and journals dating back to the 17th century. Every publication issued by any state agency is stored here, along with town, city, and county reports. In addition, there is an extensive collection of statutory laws and judicial decisions of all the forty-nine other states and a complete collection of current federal laws.

The State Library is a depository library for material on the history of Massachusetts and its towns and cities. While the library is open for research on the premises to anyone, only certain state employees have borrowing privileges—and even these are limited.

Finally, the upstairs reading area contains stacks of newspapers from large and small cities and towns all over the state.

INDEX

INDEX